PAPER BOX

is bursting with ingenious, fun thing
how to design and create your own
modeling in papier mâché and disc
money-saving ideas for gift-wrap a
of different ways of printing too, from simple potato prints to
lino cuts. All you need is a few tools, a little imagination – and
PAPER BOX!

Also available in Knight Books:

PUPPET BOX
Juliet Bawden

HOW TO HALT A HICCUP AND OTHER HANDY HINTS
Mary Danby

THE RAINY DAY SURVIVAL BOOK
Jeremy Tapscott

DIRTY, LOUD AND BRILLIANT
Carol Vorderman

PAPER BOX

JULIET BAWDEN

ILLUSTRATED BY MANDY JOHNS

KNIGHT BOOKS
HODDER AND STOUGHTON

Copyright © 1990 by Albury Technical Services

First published in Great Britain in 1991 by Knight Books

This book is sold subject to the condition that it shall not, by way of trade or otherwise, be lent, re-sold, hired out or otherwise circulated without the publisher's prior consent in any form of binding or cover other than that in which it is published and without a similar condition including this condition being imposed on the subsequent purchaser.

No part of this publication may be reproduced or transmitted in any form or by any means, electronically or mechanically, including photocopying, recording or any information storage or retrieval system, without either the prior permission in writing from the publisher or a licence, permitting restricted copying. In the United Kingdom such licences are issued by the Copyright Licensing Agency, 33–34 Alfred Place, London WC1E 7DP.

British Library Cataloguing in Publication Data
Bawden, Juliet
Paperbox
1. Paper
I. Title. II. Johns, Mand
676

ISBN 0 340 53953 4

Printed and bound in Great Britain for Hodder and Stoughton Children's Books, a division of Hodder and Stoughton Ltd., Mill Road, Dunton Green, Sevenoaks, Kent TN13 2YA. (Editorial Office: 47 Bedford Square, London WC1B 3DP) by Cox & Wyman Ltd., Reading, Berks.

With thanks to

3M for providing masking tapes

UNIBOND for supplying glues

CONTENTS

- 9 Introduction
- 10 Tools and materials
- 12 General equipment
- 13 History of paper
- 15 Making paper
- 22 Making books
- 26 Paper beads
- 27 Paper earrings
- 30 Paper quilling
- 33 Paper quill jewellery
- 35 Papier mâché earrings
- 37 Two dimensional jewellery
- 38 Red Indian head-dress
- 39 Caterpillar
- 40 Bird mobile
- 42 Paper doll chains
- 43 Buried treasure map
- 44 Magic message
- 45 Magic picture
- 46 Paper weaving
- 48 Cones
- 50 Gift tags
- 52 Paper cup
- 53 Paper box
- 54 Hat box or box hat?
- 56 Papier mâché models
- 58 A useful pot or vase
- 59 Papier mâché beads
- 60 Roller prints
- 63 Brass rubbing
- 64 Patterning tissues
- 65 Making a collage
- 67 Block prints
- 68 Potato prints
- 70 Wooden block prints
- 71 Easy stencils
- 73 Making and using stencils
- 76 Lino printing
- 80 Marbling paper
- 82 Decorating paper
- 85 Paper cuts
- 87 Decoupage
- 88 Silhouettes
- 90 Paper plate masks
- 91 Papier mâché helmet
- 93 Paper costumes
- 98 Book plates
- 99 Paper flowers
- 100 Perfumed papers
- 101 Cat pencil holder
- 102 Christmas cards
- 106 Paper hats
- 107 Paper crackers
- 108 Wrap it up

INTRODUCTION

Paper is wonderful stuff! Which is why I've written this book. It is all around us. We use it for so many things from packaging, reading and writing, and for making things. It is used for stamps, banknotes, computers, cooking and you can probably think of even more uses. This book tells you a little of the history of paper. It shows you how to make and decorate paper. It even shows you how to use waste paper. As a craft material it is great because you don't need too many tools with which to work, so you can just get on and do it without having to spend a fortune.

Some of the projects do use tools which are potentially dangerous so do take great care when using craft knives and matches. Get a grown-up to help you if you are in any doubt.

I hope you enjoy reading the book and making lots of the things in it.

TOOLS AND MATERIALS

There are three types of paper: hand-made, mould-made and machine-made. Hand-made papers have no grain. The grain is the way in which the fibres lie. In hand-made papers they are all higgledy-piggledy.

If you want to tear paper it is easier to do this along the grain of the paper. To find out which way the grain runs, curl the paper first in one direction and then the other. You will find that one way bends more easily than the other. The easiest way will be the way in which the grain runs.

There are many kinds of paper, with very different uses from one another:

TISSUE PAPER is a thin paper. It is often used for gift wrapping and protecting china objects. It can be brightly coloured and is translucent.

CREPE PAPER is stretchy in feel and slightly wrinkled in appearance. It is good for making decorations which may need to stretch slightly and for making fancy dress costumes.

TRACING PAPER, sometimes known as greaseproof paper, is transparent and used mainly for laying over an image to transfer the image on to another piece of paper.

CARBON PAPER can also be used for transferring images. It is impregnated with ink.

RICE PAPER is made from rice and generally used in cooking, although it is also used in Japanese watercolours.

CARTRIDGE PAPER is a printing paper which comes in a variety of thicknesses and qualities, usually white.

BLOTTING PAPER is a very soft paper with long fibres; very good for papier mâché.

FOIL PAPER has a metallic finish.

EMBOSSED PAPER has a raised surface or pattern running through it. Often flocked and used as wallpaper.

GENERAL EQUIPMENT

These are most of the things you will need to make the designs in this book, but an equipment list is given at the beginning of each project.

PENCILS – from Hs (hard pencils) to Bs (soft pencils), B6 being extremely soft.

PENCIL SHARPENER

CRAFT KNIFE – with spare blades; sharp edges get blunt on paper fairly quickly.

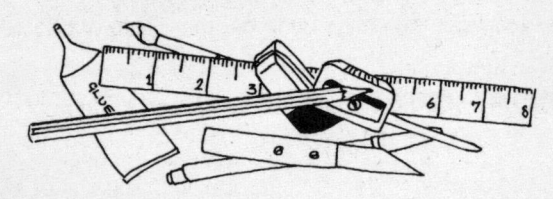

PAPER-CUTTING SCISSORS – get these in both small and large sizes if you can afford to, the large for cutting big areas, the small for cutting out details.

ADHESIVE – glue sticks are good for quick neat jobs. Wall paper paste or poly vinyl acetate are useful for papier mâché.

PENCIL ERASER
RULER
PROTRACTOR
COMPASS
STICKYTAPE
INVISIBLE TAPE
MASKING TAPE
CUTTING EDGE
DRAWING BOARD
PAPER CUTTING BOARD
FELT TIPS
PAINTS AND BRUSHES

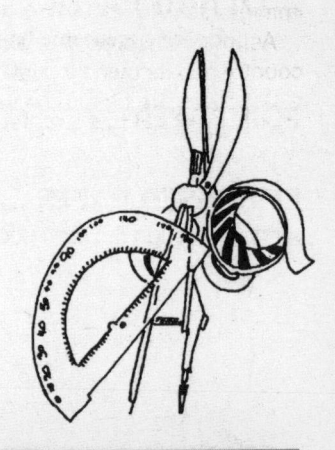

HISTORY OF PAPER

The earliest kind of paper was papyrus which was made from a grass-like plant, "Cyperus papyrus", from which the word paper is derived. This was used by the ancient Egyptians.

In other parts of the world paper was made from different substances. In central America the Mayans used a bark-like paper to write on. In the Pacific fine bark paper and paper made from cloth was used and in the Far East "rice paper" was developed.

Paper as we know it today came to the western world from China, where it is said to have been invented in the second century AD.

Knowledge of paper making spread along the trade routes through Korea, Japan and Nepal and by the ninth century it had reached India. In the eighth century, paper making travelled to the Arab world via Africa, and in the twelfth century paper making began in Europe, in Spain first of all, and then France, Italy, Germany, Switzerland, Portugal and Holland. In the thirteenth century watermarks were invented in Italy. A watermark is a translucent design that can be seen when the paper is held up to the light. Watermarks usually show the name of the maker and sometimes the date when the paper was made. It was not until the fifteenth century that paper making was first recorded in England while in America it appears to have coincided with the settling of European immigrants.

As the craft spread, so did the different techniques. Each country had its own innovations. but the usual tool of paper making was the mould, on which a mat of fibres was laid to create sheets of paper.

HOW PAPER IS MADE

In both Europe and the Far East, traditionally paper was made from hemp or recycled cotton rags. Both of these substances have exceptionally long fibres and this helps to hold the paper together. To make the fibres into paper they must first be broken down and separated. This is done by boiling them in caustic substances. They are then beaten and pounded until the fibres are soft enough to form a soft matted layer when placed on a mould. When this layer is dry it will be paper.

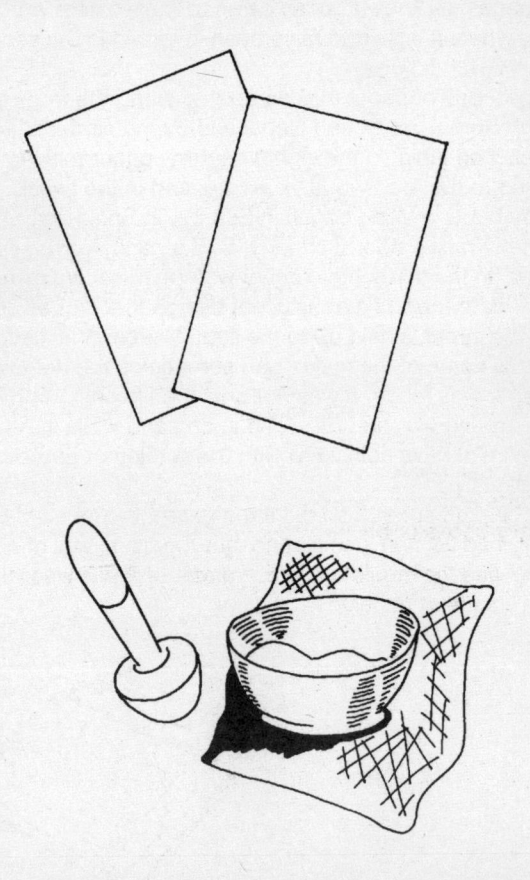

MAKING PAPER

The method described here is not for making paper from scratch but a way of recycling old paper and introducing new fibres to create hand-made paper. When using paper to recycle, avoid newspaper if possible as it has a high acid content which can turn the paper brown quickly.

Computer paper, typing paper, egg boxes, serviettes, may all be put to good use and pulped.

Paper making does need quite a lot of equipment and you may need help from a grown-up.

YOU WILL NEED

- old paper for recycling
- a food blender (liquidiser)
- large oblong washing up bowl
- 2 small silk screen frames which will fit horizontally into the oblong basin; one frame should be stretched with curtain netting (the mould), the other left as a screen (the deckle)
- some bits of old blanket
- J-cloths
- plastic sheeting to cover the surrounding areas and floor as it can be rather wet and messy
- lots of clean newspaper
- 2 wooden boards
- palette knife
- heavy books or bricks

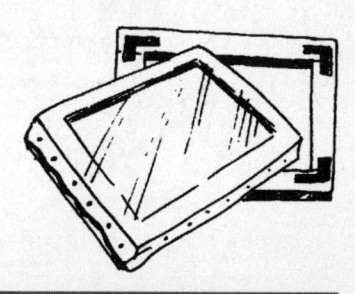

INSTRUCTIONS

There are various processes for paper making and each one is described below. Before using the blender or liquidiser, do ask permission and if possible have an adult around to assist. You shouldn't need the blender on for more than a minute at a time. If the machine starts to labour *switch it off* and remove some of the paper.

PREPARING THE PULP

1 Tear or rip up the pieces of paper into shreds about the size of postage stamps.

2 Fill the blender 3/4 full of water and add approximately 40 pieces of paper for every 2 pints of water (fig 1).

3 Switch the blender on.

4 When the paper is pulped pour it into the washing up bowl (fig 1).

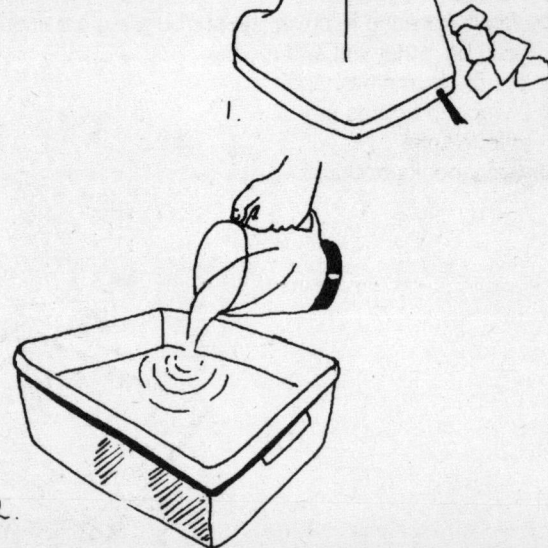

MAKING THE SHEET OF PAPER

1 Stir the pulp with your hands to distribute the fibres evenly.

2 Put the deckle over the mould with the outside edges lined up.

3 Hold the deckle and the mould together by their long sides, and lower the whole thing very gently into the bowl until it is horizontal.

4 Lift the mould and deckle out of the water: they will be full of very liquid pulp.

5 Hold the mould and deckle horizontally above the water and let the excess water drain away (fig 3).

6 Supporting the underside of the mould with one hand remove the deckle, being careful not to let it damage the edge of the paper (fig 4).

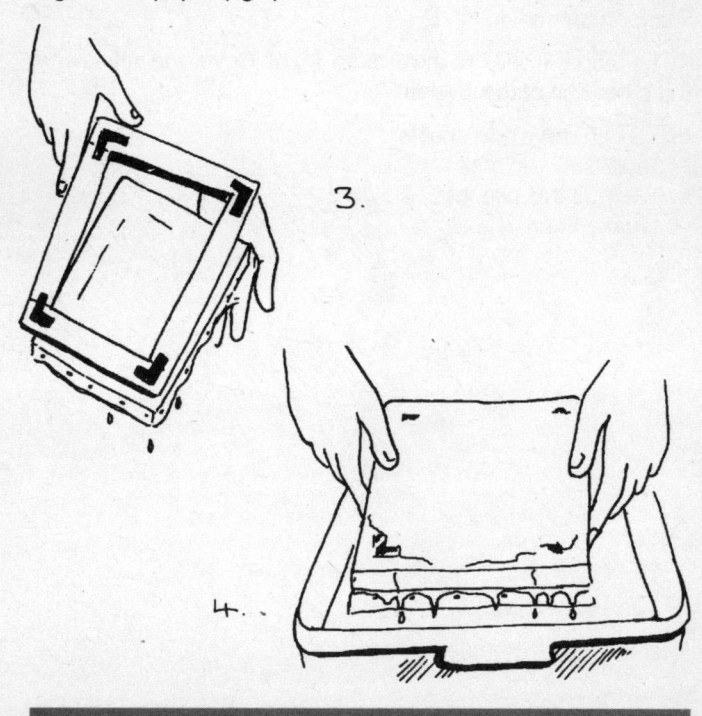

COUCHING

This means turning the wet pulp on to a base on which it will dry.

INSTRUCTIONS

1 Cut up the old blanket and arrange the pieces in a small soft mound, slightly larger than the sheet of paper you are making.

2 Cover the mound with a J-cloth.

3 Rest the edge of the mould on the edge of the J-cloth and turn it so the pulped paper lies on top of the J-cloth. Press firmly before lifting off the mould (fig 5).

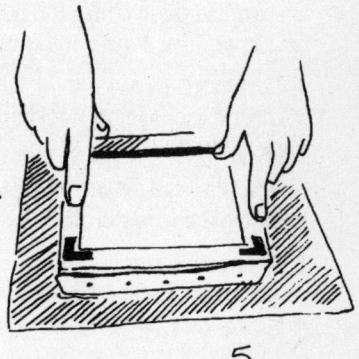

4 The pulp will stick to the J-cloth (fig 6). Cover the sheet with the other half of the J-cloth.

5 You can more add sheets of paper with J-cloths between to this pile, as you make them.

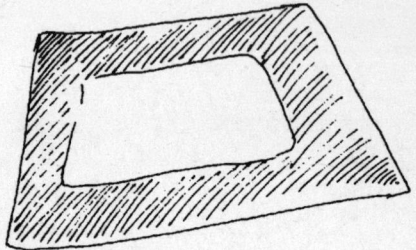

PRESSING

1 Cover the floor with something to protect it. This process is messy.

2 Lay the pile of couched sheets of paper and their cloths between three or four newspapers.

3 Place this between two boards and then stand on top of the pile (fig 7). The water will be squeezed out.

DRYING

You must let the paper dry at its own pace or it may warp.

1 Remove the pile of cloths from the newspapers.

2 Layer the J-cloths and paper between new layers of newspaper of three or four sheets thickness each time (fig 8).

3 Stand this new pile on one board with another on top of it and cover with heavy books or bricks (fig 9).

4 Repeat steps 1-2 every 6 hours until the cloths and paper are completely dry. This may take up to a day.

5 When the paper is dry open the cloths and remove the paper with a palette knife (figs 10 and 11).

10.

11.

To make special effects, add any of the following to the white pulp: hair cuttings, grass, leaves, coloured pulped paper, mushroom skins or anything else you wish to experiment with. The results will probably be unusual and pretty.

You can add strips of paper, for example tissue paper, at the couching stage so that they become embedded as the paper dries (fig 12 and 13).

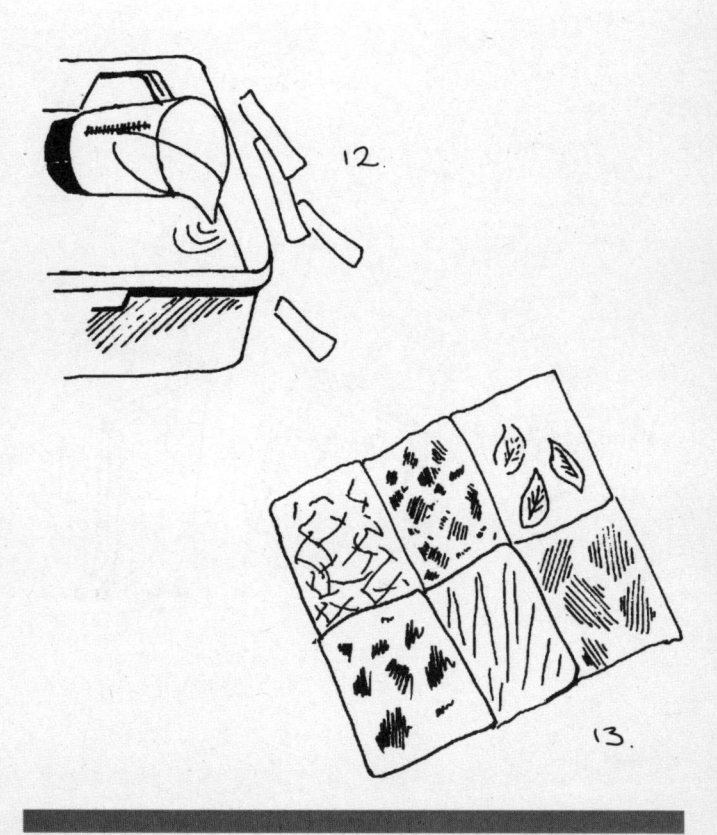

MAKING BOOKS

When books are made commercially they are first printed on long sheets of paper from an offset press. When all the sheets have been printed they are then bound, but before that they have to be folded, separated into "signatures" and folded again. The diagram below shows how a signature is composed. The pages are printed in this order so that when they are folded they will appear in the correct order.

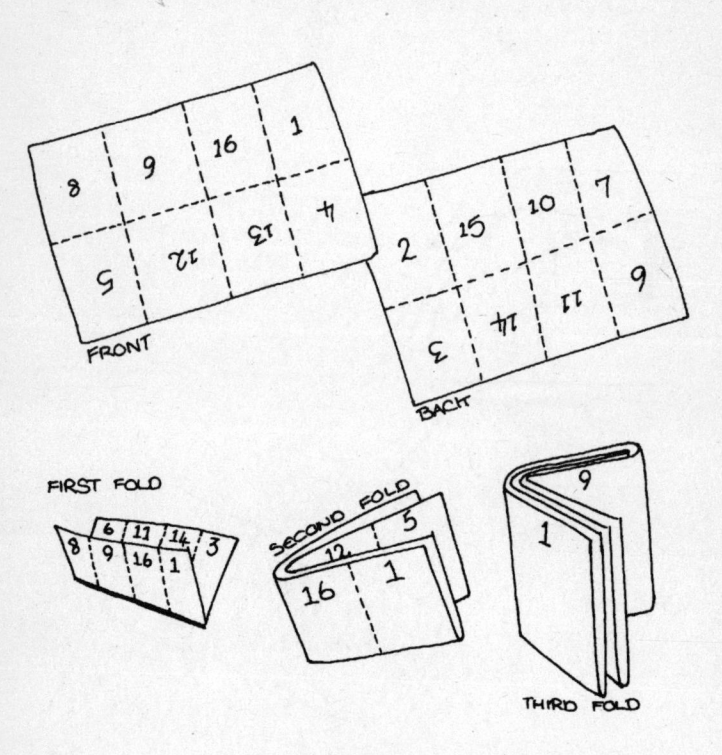

HAND-BINDING

To hand-bind a book, a set of signatures is aligned in the correct order. The backs are then sewn together and glue is applied to hold the signatures together. A lining, called bookbinder's mull, is glued to the spine and the case (cover) is glued to the lining.

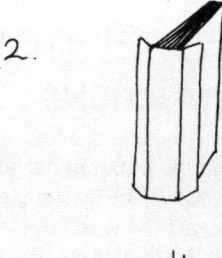

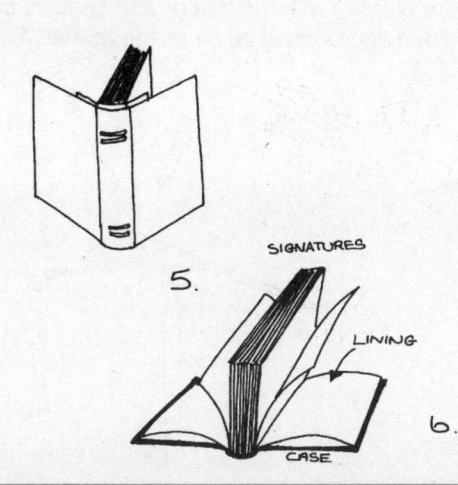

MAKE YOUR OWN BOOK

YOU WILL NEED

- paper (typing paper will do)
- strong knife for cutting
- surface on which to cut
- needle
- linen thread (you can use embroidery skein if you can't find linen thread)
- straight-edged scissors
- ruler
- pencil
- felt tips and plain paper for a cover, or decorative paper.

INSTRUCTIONS

1 Fold the paper in halves and quarters or even eighths until the book is the size you require. Remember the book is going to be half the width it is now, when you fold the paper to make the final book. Each folded piece of paper will make one section of the book. You may only want one section or you may wish to add others.

2 When you are pleased with the size of your section, then slit it along the folded edge almost as far as the "gutter" fold (fig 1).

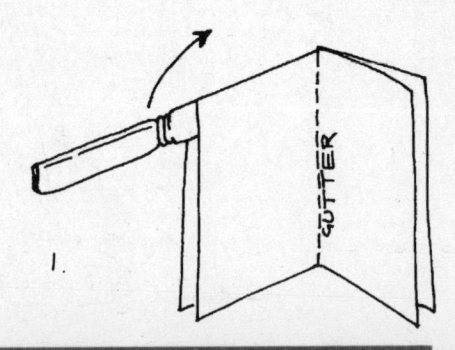

3 To sew each section together, use the needle to pierce an odd number of evenly spaced holes down the gutter. Make sure each hole goes through every layer of paper.

4 Take a length of thread two and a half times the length of the gutter and thread it on to the needle.

5 Sew the section together by sewing through the holes you made (fig 2).

6 When the section is sewn, continue the slit at the top of the page to the gutter and trim the rest with the scissors.

7 Make a cover by taking a piece of coloured paper or plain paper you will decorate later. Cut the paper to 10cm higher than your book and three times its width.

8 Fold the paper in half and wrap it round the book. Cut V shapes at the spine and corners (fig 3) and fold to cover the book.

9 Cut a [shape on the last page of the left hand side of the book and a] on the last page of the right hand side of the book; this will hold the paper in place.

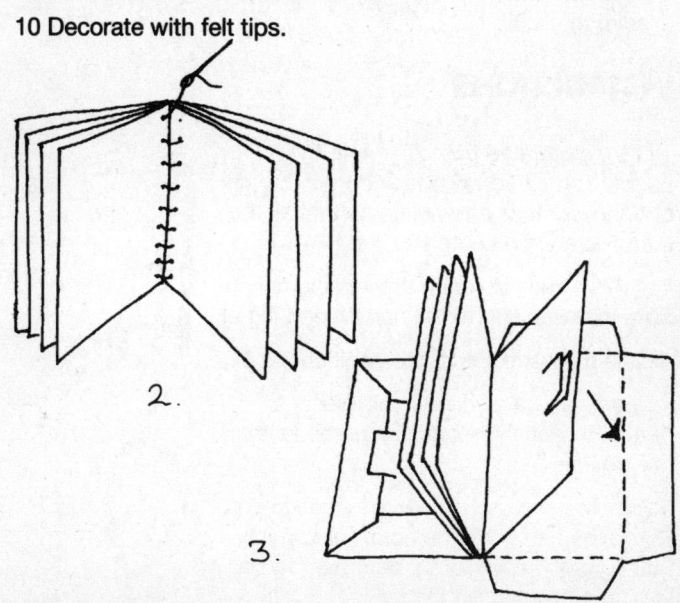

10 Decorate with felt tips.

2.

3.

PAPER BEADS

This is a very cheap and easy way to produce beads for necklaces or bracelets. Use old wrapping paper, birthday cards, magazines or even newspaper. You can also use plain paper and decorate each bead before varnishing.

YOU WILL NEED

- paper or card
- pencil
- ruler
- scissors
- knitting needle
- glue
- Plasticine
- paints or coloured felt tips
- clear varnish
- shirring elastic

INSTRUCTIONS

1 Draw elongated triangles on to the paper. You can draw one and then cut this out and use it as a template so that all the triangles are the same size (fig 1).

2 Cut out and roll round the knitting needle from the wide end to the narrow end (fig 2).

3 Glue the narrow end into position (fig 3).

4 When you have made a number of beads, thread them back on to the knitting needle.

5 Rest the end of the needle in the lump of Plasticine and paint the beads or varnish them (fig 4). Leave to dry before threading on to shirring elastic (fig 5).

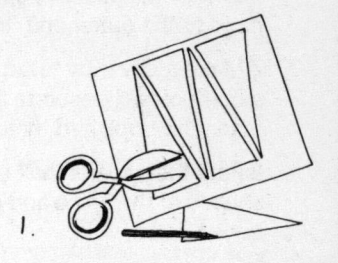

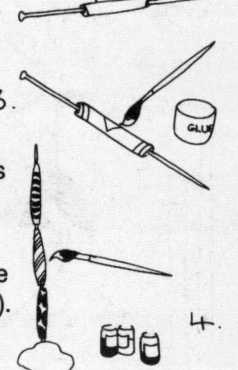

PAPER EARRINGS

YOU WILL NEED

- tracing paper
- pencil
- cartridge paper
- felt tips
- scissors
- Pritt stick or another glue
- needle
- jump ring and earring findings

INSTRUCTIONS

1 Trace the design above.

2 Transfer it on to cartridge paper.

3 Colour in with felt tips.

4 Cut out along the outside edge and fold lengthways along the dotted lines A-B, C-D, E-F, G-H (fig 1).

5 Fold tabs A-C, B-D, E-G, F-H, N-O, P-Q, along dotted lines, then fold tabs G-E and D-F.

6 Glue all the tabs and stick into place as in fig 2

7 Pierce the hole with a needle and hang from a jump ring

8 Attach the jump ring to a jewellery finding.

2.

To make the earrings on this page, follow steps 1-3 on page 27. Then fold along the lines as you did before, fold in the tabs and stick together. Attach a jewellery finding.

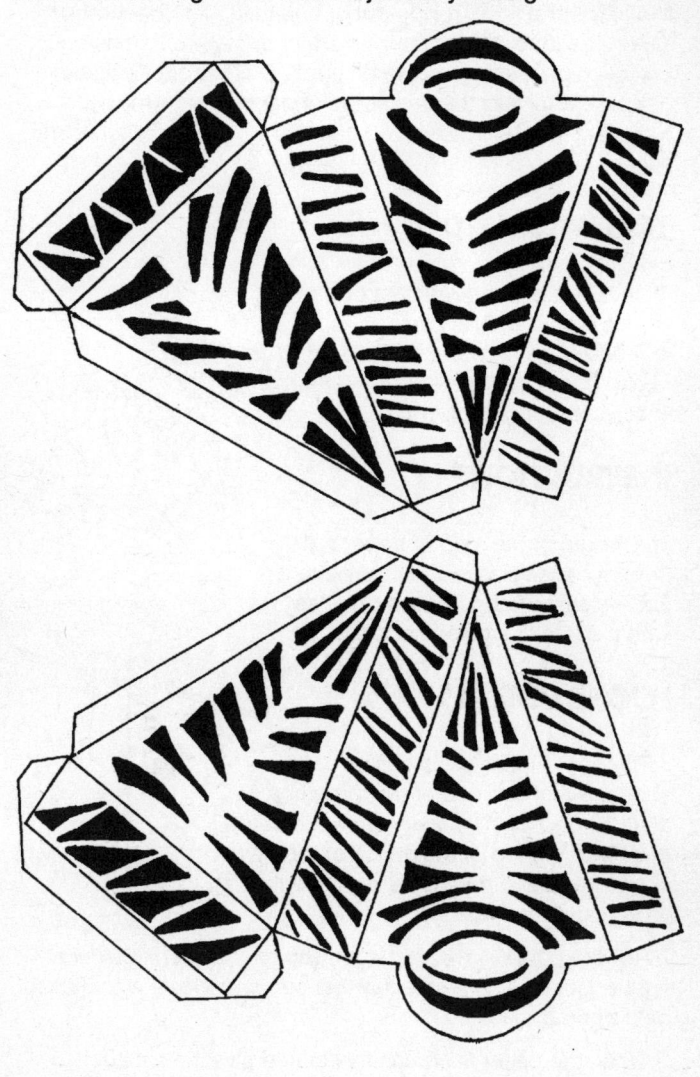

PAPER QUILLING

Quilling is the art of rolling paper and using it to decorate. It can be used to make paper jewellery or picture frames or it can even be used to create pictures. Quilling got its name because originally the thin strips of paper were wrapped around quills. Nowadays you can use a hair grip or a cocktail stick.

YOU WILL NEED

- coloured paper streamers or paper
- glue – glue stick is ideal.
- round nosed jewellers' pliers, or a hair grip or cocktail stick
- scissors for cutting ends

INSTRUCTIONS

The length of the strip of paper will determine the size of the final pattern. For experimental purposes practise with a 20cm (8 in) piece of paper.

LOOSE COIL (1)

1 This is the most basic quilled shape. Place one end of the streamer in a hair grip (fig 1), making sure that it lies level with the top of the grip. Rotate the grip in one hand and roll the paper on to it using the thumb and forefinger of the other hand.

2 Roll the paper slowly to begin with so that it spirals quite tightly. Check all the time that the coil is still level with the top of the grip.

3 When the paper is completely curled give it a squeeze to help to hold it together before taking it off the grip.

4 Hold the coil gently with one hand and remove the grip with the other. This may mean that you have to loosen the coil a little (fig 2).

5 Ease the coil to the size that you desire and then stick the loose end on to the coil to keep it in position.

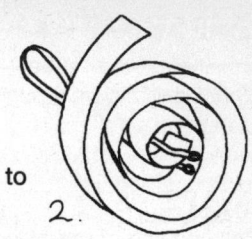

LOOSE OPEN COIL

This is made in the same way as a loose coil but the end is left to spring free (fig 3).

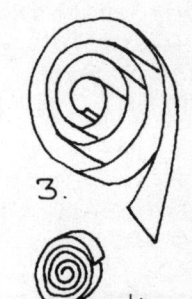

TIGHT COIL

This coil is stuck before removing from the grip so that it is extremely tight (fig 4).

TEAR DROP

Made like the loose coil. After sticking the end, pinch one side to a point so that it is teardrop shape (fig 5).

EYE SHAPE

Made as tear drop, but both ends are pinched (fig 6).

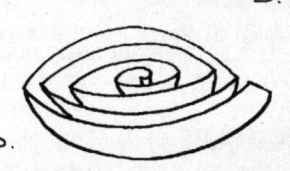

LEAF SHAPE

Like the eye shape but more elongated and pinched with gentle curves in opposite directions (fig 7).

SHAPE

Roll one end of the strip to just over half way. Turn the strip over and roll the other end. Roll it in the same direction to just over half way. Let it spring free. No glueing is necessary (fig 8).

SCROLL

The same as S but with both coils on the same side of the strip. Again no adhesive is necessary (fig 9).

HEART

Similar to scroll, but the strip is creased in half first (fig 10).

V-SHAPE

Exactly the same as the heart, but coiling away from the inside of the crease (fig 11).

PAPER QUILL JEWELLERY BOARD

Before making this jewellery it is a good idea to make a surface on which to work.

YOU WILL NEED

- a small board or piece of card (the back of a cornflakes packet will do).
- thin piece of foam large enough to cover the card
- piece of greaseproof or tracing paper
- stapler

1 Cover the board in foam and put the tracing paper on top of the foam.

2 Staple the sandwich together at the corners.

PAPER QUILL JEWELLERY

YOU WILL NEED

- pencil and paper
- a board (instructions above)
- paper quills (p 30)
- pins with large heads
- glue
- jewellery findings (rings, chains, loops, etc)
- varnish (this may be clear nail varnish)

INSTRUCTIONS

1 Draw a design and slip it under the tracing paper.

2 Make quills (p30) to fit on to your design.

3 Lay the first quill on the design and pin it through its centre into place (fig 1).

4 Glue along one side of another quill and lay it alongside the first quill. Pin this into place through its centre (fig 2).

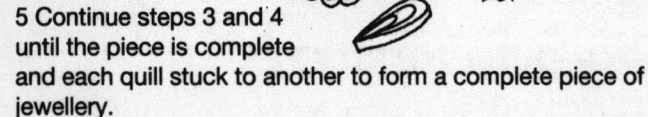

5 Continue steps 3 and 4 until the piece is complete and each quill stuck to another to form a complete piece of jewellery.

6 When the piece is thoroughly dry, remove the pins and coat with varnish.

7 Stick on any beads etc you may wish and attach to the jewellery findings (fig 3).

PAPIER MÂCHÉ EARRINGS

From this basic method you can make all kinds of jewellery. One balloon will create enough papier mâché to make lots of earrings or other pieces of jewellery.

YOU WILL NEED

- balloon
- thread
- shirring elastic
- wallpaper paste
- newspaper
- scissors
- clear Fablon
- jewellery findings

INSTRUCTIONS

1 Blow up the balloon and tie a knot in it. Tie a piece of thread around the knot. Following the maker's instructions, mix the wallpaper paste to the consistency of double cream (fig 1).

2 Rip newspaper into pieces approximately 2cm (³/₄ in) square. Dip a piece of paper into the glue, and stick it on to the balloon, smoothing it into position. Repeat this process with the next piece of paper overlapping the first piece as you stick it in position (fig 2).

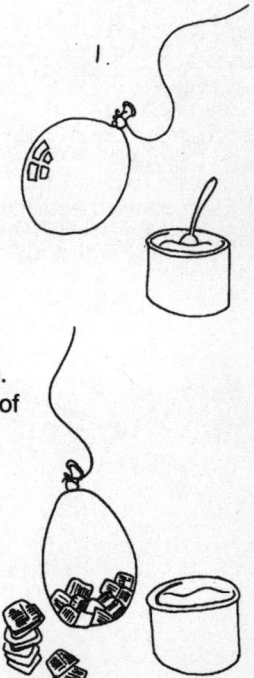

3 Cover the balloon with paper, overlapping each piece until the balloon is completely covered. Make sure that each piece is smoothed into position. Leave the thread free and hang the balloon in a doorway or under a window sill to dry overnight (fig 3).

4 The following day cover the balloon in another layer of paper and leave this to dry. Altogether you will need to cover the balloon eight times, allowing each layer to dry before applying the next.

5 When the eight layers are dry either undo the knot on the balloon or pop it with a pin. Cut the papier mâché balloon in half and use each half to cut lots of different shapes for earrings (fig 4).

6 When you have cut your basic shape, cover it with clear Fablon to protect it.

7 Pierce each shape with a pin and attach a jump ring (fig 5). Hang this from a kidney wire and wear!

TWO DIMENSIONAL JEWELLERY

YOU WILL NEED

- a copy of your favourite comic
- black card
- clear Fablon
- scissors
- glue
- brooch back or tie-pin back or earclips or kidney hooks

INSTRUCTIONS

1 Cut out the bit of the newspaper you would like to make into a piece of jewellery (fig 1).

2 Stick it on to black card (fig 2).

3 Cover the front and back with clear Fablon (fig 3).

4 Either pierce a hole from which to hang the earring or stick on to a brooch back or tie-pin (fig 4).

RED INDIAN HEAD-DRESS

YOU WILL NEED

- thin card, corrugated is a good idea
- ruler
- pencil
- scissors
- crayons, felt tips or paint and brush
- sticky tape

INSTRUCTIONS

1 Draw twelve feathers on the card about 15cm (6 in) high.

2 Cut out the shapes and then colour them in (fig 1).

3 Fringe the edges by cutting slits in the sides with scissors. This will make them look feathery.

4 Cut a piece of card long enough to fit round your head with a little left over as an overlap. Decorate this with bright patterns.

5 Tape the feathers to the inside of the head band, or if you are using corrugated paper, stick the feathers down the holes (fig 2).

6 Join the headband by sticking the two ends together with tape (fig 3).

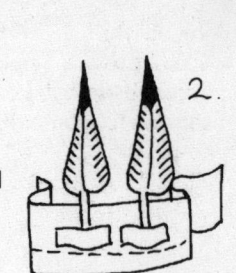

CATERPILLAR

YOU WILL NEED

- cardboard egg boxes
- green and yellow paint
- shirring elastic
- needle

INSTRUCTIONS

1 Separate the bits of egg boxes.

2 Paint half the bits green and half yellow. Leave to dry.

3 Paint or draw eyes on to one of the egg boxes (fig 2).

4 Using the shirring elastic and needle, thread through the centres of the boxes, first a green, and then a yellow, and so on (fig 3).

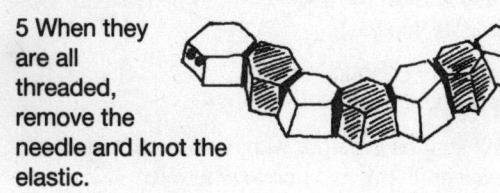

5 When they are all threaded, remove the needle and knot the elastic.

IDEAS Other animals like the drawings below.

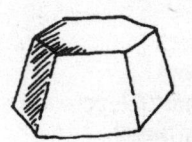

BIRD MOBILE

YOU WILL NEED

- tracing paper
- pencil
- scissors
- felt tips
- thin card
- tissue paper
- 2 wire coat hangers
- glue stick
- button thread

INSTRUCTIONS

1 Trace each bird you need twice on to card (fig 1). You need two bird shapes to make one bird and you can make as many birds as you wish for each mobile.

2 Cut out the two birds.

3 Glue the two bird shapes together with a piece of thread sandwiched in between them, just above where it says wing (make the thread different lengths on each bird – this will make a more interesting mobile) (fig 2).

4 Cut the wing slit.

5 To make fanned wings cut a piece of tissue paper 35 x 22cm (14 x 9 in), concertina the paper lengthways and then make the edges round using scissors.

6 Push the wing through the slit, so there are equal amounts on either side of the body, and fan out the wings (fig 3).

7 To make the tail, cut a piece of tissue paper 35 x 12cm (14 x 5 in) and concertina it width ways. Stick one end over the tail of the cardboard bird and fan out the tail (fig 4).

8 Decorate each bird with lots of patterns, making them as bright and jolly as possible.

9 To make the mobile, push one coat hanger into the other to form a cross and tie into a knot at the top. Hang the birds from the cross (fig 5).

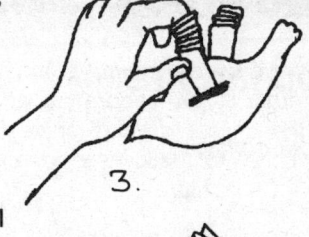

PAPER DOLL CHAINS

These are easy to make and may be used as cards or for decorating at a birthday or Christmas. You can make dolls or bats or witches for Hallowe'en, or snowmen or Santas for Christmas.

YOU WILL NEED

- paper
- pencil and scissors
- pens or crayons if you are going to decorate

INSTRUCTIONS

1 Fold a piece of paper into even pleats (fig 1).

2 Draw the doll or whatever shape you want, being careful to leave one place on each side where it joins the edge; this is usually the arms (fig 2).

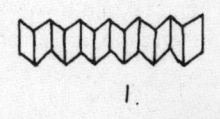

3 Cut out the shape, being careful not to cut through the arms or other bits touching the side of the folds (fig 3).

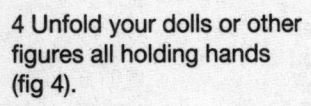

4 Unfold your dolls or other figures all holding hands (fig 4).

5 Decorate them and hang them up.

BURIED TREASURE MAP

YOU WILL NEED

- brown paint, brush and water
- saucer
- sheet of white or cream coloured paper
- waterproof felt tip pens or a quill (large feather) and a bottle of ink
- matches (and a grown-up around in case things get out of hand!)
- cord or string

INSTRUCTIONS

1 Mix the brown paint in a saucer with lots of water so that you have a "wash".

2 Paint the wash on to the paper and leave it to dry. The paper should now be an oldish looking colour.

3 Either draw the map in felt tips or use the quill and ink (this will be scratchier and more authentic looking).

4 Now being very careful and with a grown-up there and in a place where you cannot set fire to anything (over a sink is good), light a match and very carefully scorch the edge of the paper. Blow the match out before you burn your fingers or most of the map. You should end up with a pleasantly uneven scorched edge.

5 Roll the map up and tie with a piece of cord or string.

MAGIC MESSAGE

This is another trick for you to show your friends.

YOU WILL NEED

- white paper
- lemon juice
- paint brush
- an iron and ironing board
- an adult to assist with the ironing

INSTRUCTIONS

1 Dip the paint brush in the lemon juice and write your message on the paper.

2 As the juice dries the message will disappear.

3 To find out what the message says, plug in the iron on a low temperature setting and iron over the message. It will slowly appear brown and be clear enough to read.

MAGIC PICTURE

Make a picture appear from nowhere!

YOU WILL NEED

- white cartridge paper
- pencil
- masking tape
- white poster paint
- waterproof black Indian ink

INSTRUCTIONS

1 Draw your picture lightly in pencil.

2 Tape the picture to a board and fill in the picture with white poster paint, Leave this to dry (fig 1).

3 When the paint is dry cover the whole of the paper with black ink and leave this to dry.

4 Now run cold water over the page and the ink will come off revealing the picture below (fig 2).

PAPER WEAVING 1 - Place mats

These mats are very easy to make and are effective and fun especially if you are having a party.

YOU WILL NEED

- paper in two or more colours
- scissors
- glue stick
- ruler and pencil

INSTRUCTIONS

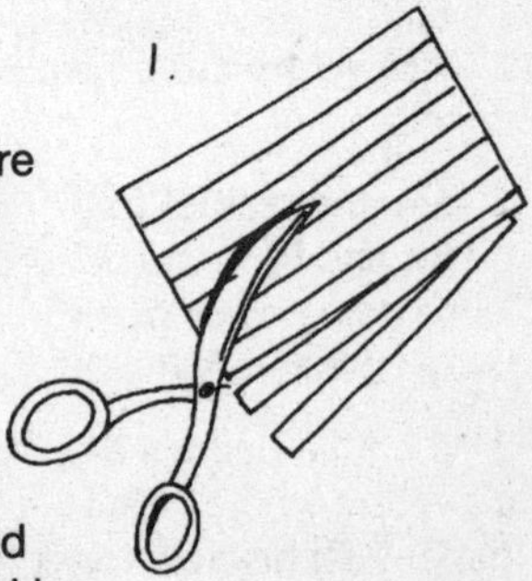

1 Using the pencil and ruler, measure strips along your paper 2.5cm (1 in) wide and 30cm (12 in) long.

2 Cut out the strips of paper (fig 1).

3 Lay ten strips of paper flat on the table parallel to each other and begin weaving the other strips in and out starting from the centre and working to within 2.5cm (1in) from either end (fig 2).

4 Glue back the ends of each strip to finish (fig 3).

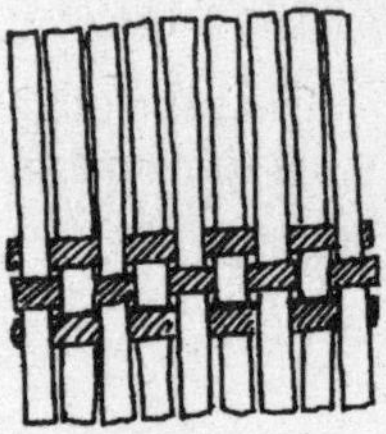

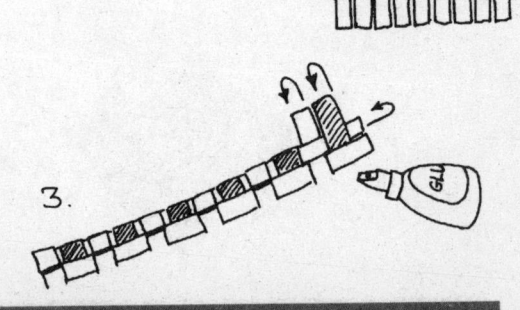

PAPER WEAVING 2

Below are various ideas for weaving with paper.

You do not have to cut strips for both the warp (the lines which go from top to bottom) and the weft (the lines which go from right to left). From a square of paper leave a border of 5cm (2 in) round the edge and cut straight lines or wavy lines or zigzag lines within the border (fig1).

Weave thin or thick wavy pieces through the lines you have cut. Experiment until you get an effect you like. Try mixing colours, or only using one colour, and see the different results (figs 2 and 3).

Try weaving using ripped paper (fig 4) of different colours, and introduce a third colour in the form of a background on which to stick the weaving.

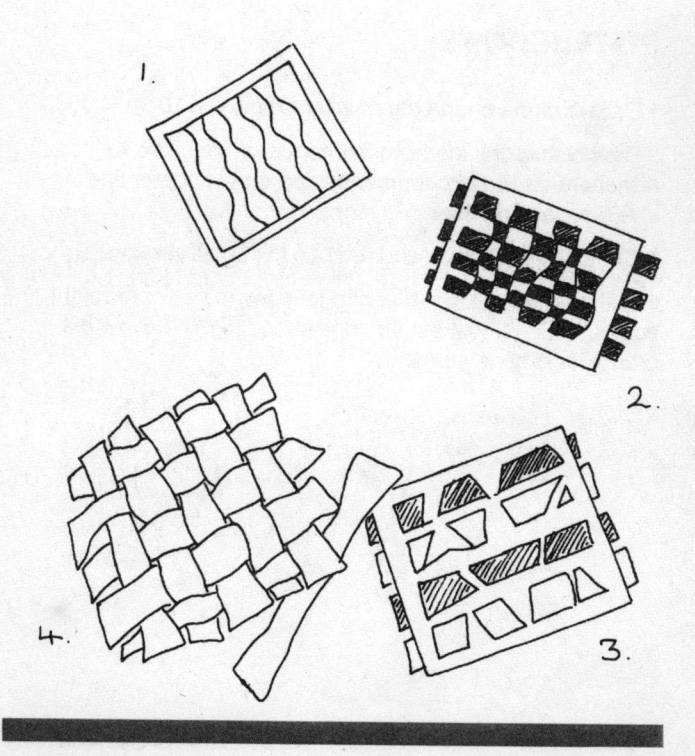

CONES

A cone is constructed from part of a circle. It is a very useful shape for making all sorts of things from hats, paper flowers and Christmas decorations to useful things such as lamp shades.

YOU WILL NEED

- a stiff piece of paper 20cm x 25cm (8 in x 10 in)
- pair of compasses
- ruler
- pencil
- protractor
- scissors
- sticky tape

INSTRUCTIONS

1 Draw a circle on the paper with a radius of 10cm (4 in).

2 Draw a straight line from the centre of the circle to anywhere on the circumference and draw another line at 90° to the first line.

3 Cut along both lines and remove the small section.

4 Pull both edges together and join down the two straight edges. This will make a fat cone shape (fig 1). Follow diagrams for other shapes.

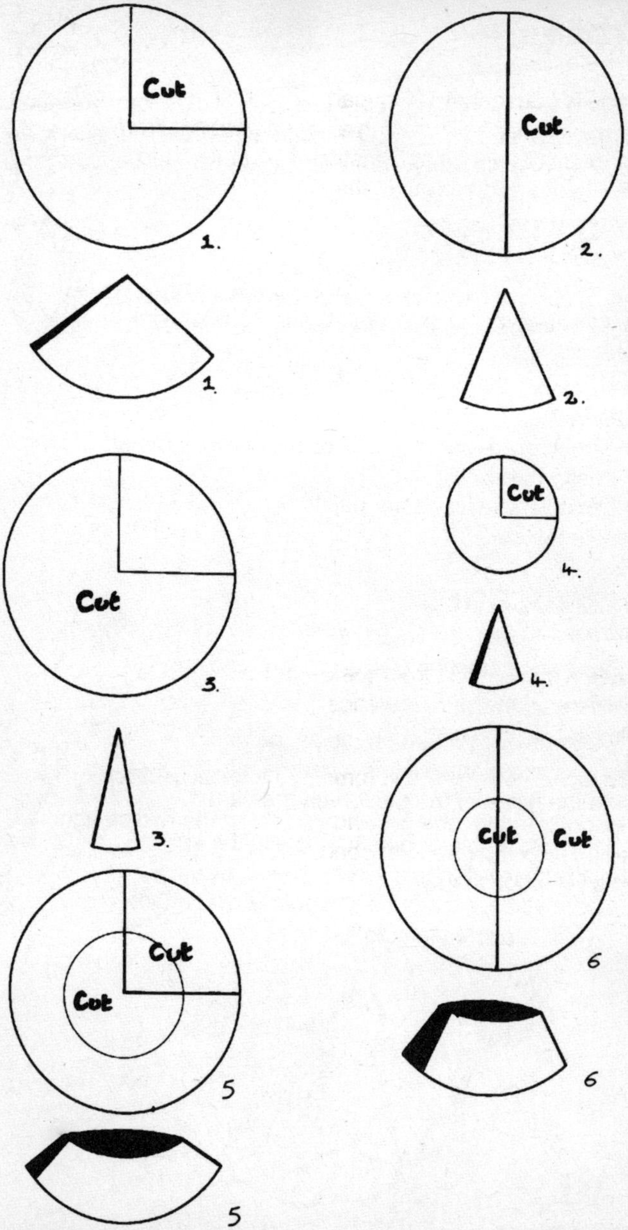
Cut
1.
Cut
2.
1.
2.
Cut
Cut
3.
4.
4.
3.
Cut
Cut
Cut
Cut
6
5
6
5

GIFT TAGS

A good way of making a present look professionally wrapped is to add a gift tag. These are quite expensive to buy and are not very original. Below are a few ideas for making your own.

YOU WILL NEED

- thin card or paper in white or various colours
- narrow ribbon, embroidery skein, or thread
- felt tip pens
- scissors

optional
- gingerbread man or teddy bear or other interesting shaped pastry cutter.
- pasta bows and poster paints
- hole punch

INSTRUCTIONS

1 Draw an interesting shape on card and cut it out.

2 Either paint a picture on the shape or features and clothes if it is a person, or write the name of the person on the card.

3 Either cut a hole or punch a hole in the top and attach the ribbon. Or draw round a pastry cutter shape. Or cut out a kite shape, and attach pasta bows to it with ribbon.

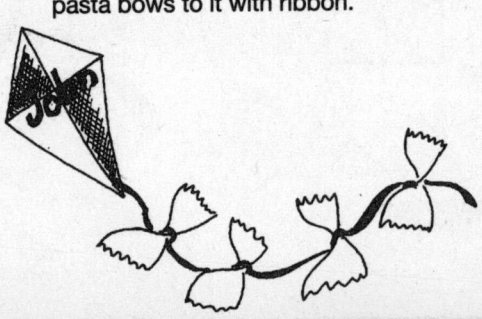

GROWN-UP GIFT TAGS

The gift tags on the previous page are great for children but you may want to make something more sophisticated for an adult.

YOU WILL NEED

- cardboard in various colours
- pencil
- scissors
- hole punch
- ribbon
- for the Valentine's day gift tag – doily, gold paint, tracing paper, glue
- for the geometric gift tag – ruler, coloured sticky tape, felt tips

INSTRUCTIONS TO MAKE A VALENTINE'S DAY GIFT TAG

1 Trace off the design below and on to red card. Punch or cut a hole where indicated.

2 Paint a doily gold and leave to dry.

3 Cut the frilly edge off the doily, gather up and stick it to the edge of the heart.

4 Add the ribbon to attach to the gift.

TO MAKE A GEOMETRIC GIFT TAG

1 Draw on to your card with a ruler a geometric shape such as a square, oblong or diamond shape.

2 Cut out the shape.

3 Either decorate with geometric designs in felt tip or stick strips of coloured tape across the tag to make an interesting design.

4 Punch a hole in the top of the card and add the ribbon or thread.

A SIMPLE PAPER CUP

This is an easy way to make a cup in an emergency. It won't last for ever but it will work and impress your friends.

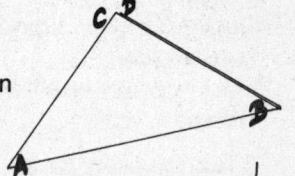

YOU WILL NEED

● a square piece of paper – not newspaper, but paper torn from a note book will do.

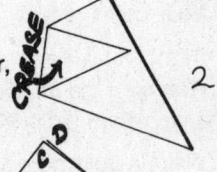

INSTRUCTIONS

1 Fold the paper in half to make a triangle (fig 1).

2 Fold point A so it is half way between points CD and B (fig 2). Crease as shown.

3 Fold point B so it is opposite point A. Crease as shown (fig 3).

4 Fold down point C and stick it between the two pieces of paper that run from A to B. Crease along the fold line.

5 Fold down point D to the back of the cup, and crease. It doesn't need to tuck in. Happy drinking.

MAKE A BOX FROM PAPER

YOU WILL NEED

- a square of cartridge paper
- scissors
- glue or stapler with staples

INSTRUCTIONS

1 Fold the paper in half (fig1).

2 Open the paper, and fold the top edge down to the crease in the centre, and the bottom edge up to the centre fold. Make crease marks where you have just folded. You now have three creases in your paper.

3 Turn the paper round so that the creases now go lengthways and repeat steps 1 and 2. Your paper will now look like fig 2.

4 Cut along the arrows from points A to B.

5 Fold in points A so they touch the nearest point C. This will make the ends of the box.

6 Stick or staple the ends into place.

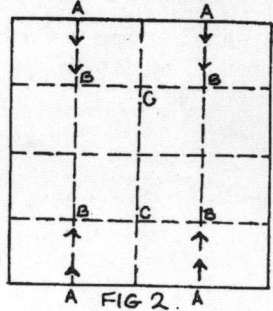

TO MAKE A LID

Follow the same instructions with a slightly larger piece of paper.

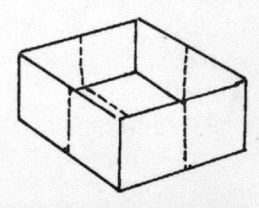

IS IT A HAT BOX OR A BOX HAT?

YOU WILL NEED

● a large square sheet of paper as big as you like

INSTRUCTIONS

1 Fold the paper in half from top to bottom. Then fold it in half from left to right to make a crease. Unfold.

2 Fold the top corners down to the centre crease (fig 1).

3 Fold the top layer A-B to the base of the triangles, then fold again over the base of the triangle (figs 2 and 3).

4 Turn the shape over and fold points C and D to the centre crease (fig 4).

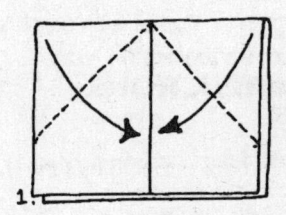

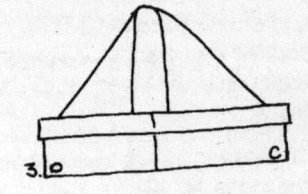

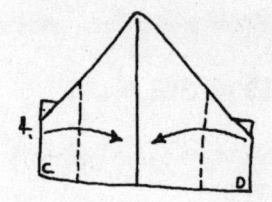

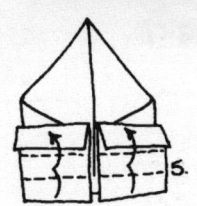

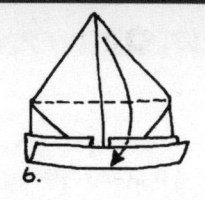

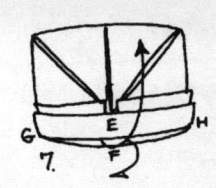

5 Turn up the bottom edge C-D twice, as you did in step 3 with A-B (fig 5).

6 Fold down the top corner and tuck it underneath all the layers at the bottom (fig 6).

7 Pull E away from F (fig 7).

8 Pull them further and further apart so that G and H come together in the middle (fig 8).

9 Flatten the shape into a square and crease the edges. Fold the right and left corners into the middle and tuck under the layers at G and H (fig 9).

10 Open the shape and square off the sides (fig 10).

11 The box (fig 11)

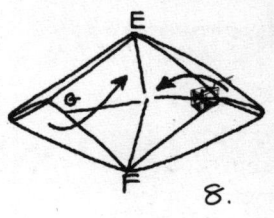

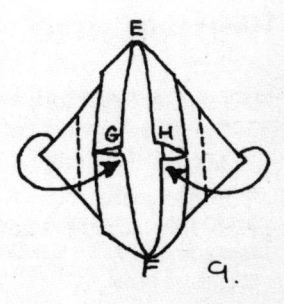

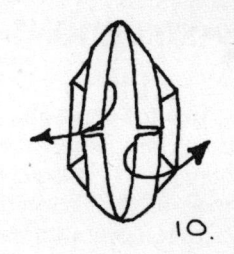

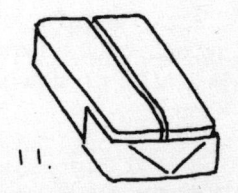

MODELS FROM PAPIER MÂCHÉ PULP

Pulped papier mâché is made from a mixture of wet paper and glue. Sometimes other things such as Polyfilla or sawdust can be added to make it heavier. Newspaper will produce a coarse pulp. Thin papers such as tissue, toilet paper and paper towels will produce a fine pulp. Keep in a plastic bag in the refrigerator or larger quantities in a plastic dustbin with a lid.

RECIPE FOR MAKING PULP

The following will make 1 quart of mash.

YOU WILL NEED

- a bucket full of torn newspaper. The pieces should be about 2.5cm (1 in) square.
- water
- old pair of tights
- small packet of wallpaper paste
- plastic bowl

INSTRUCTIONS

1 Tear the paper into pieces no larger than 2.5 cm (1 in) square. As you tear the paper, make sure it is in the direction of the grain, as it tears more easily this way. Put the paper into the bucket, cover with water and allow to soak overnight. The paper will become pulpy (fig 1).

2 Strain the paper pulp into the tights and squeeze out the surplus water (fig 2). After the pulp has been strained it will form a soft wet lump.

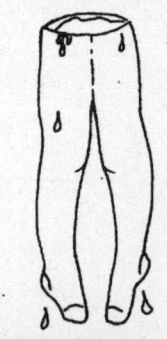

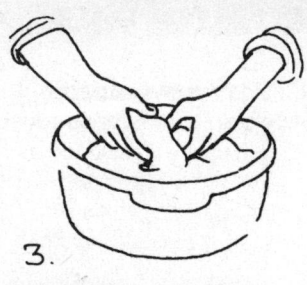

3 Mix the wallpaper paste according to the manufacturer's instructions.

4 Put the pulp in a bowl and add the paste. Mix it well with your hands (fig 3). The pulp is now ready to use.

MAKING MODELS

It is a good idea to start with small simple shapes such as mice.

YOU WILL NEED

- pulp
- newspaper
- fork and knife as modelling tools
- string or raffia for a tail
- bits of cardboard for ears

INSTRUCTIONS

1 Make and model the pulp in the same way you would clay (fig 1).

2 To make a mouse cut a small length of string and push it into the back of the model for the tail (fig 2).

3 Cut cardboard ears and stick them in the dough before it hardens (fig 3).

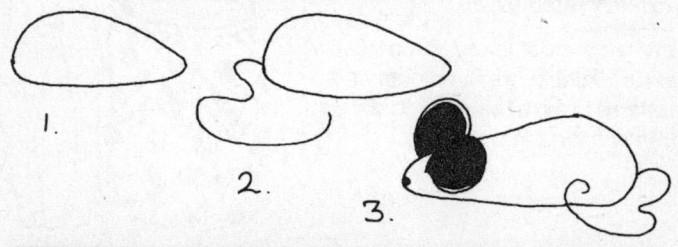

A USEFUL POT OR VASE

Because you are keeping the jam jar inside the pulp, and it is waterproof, the pot can be used for flowers.

YOU WILL NEED

- an old jam jar
- newspaper
- water
- pulp
- poster paints and brush
- clear varnish

INSTRUCTIONS

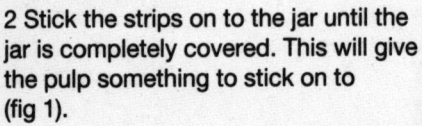

1 Rip the newspaper into strips and dunk each strip in water.

2 Stick the strips on to the jar until the jar is completely covered. This will give the pulp something to stick on to (fig 1).

3 Take a piece of pulp in your hand and stick it on to the newspaper-covered jar (fig 2).

4 Continue to add pulp until the jar is covered.

5 Leave it to dry. This may take up to a week. To help the pulp to dry, leave the pot in a warm well-ventilated room.

6 When the pot is dry, decorate it with poster paint in bright colours and patterns. Leave the paint to dry and then varnish the pot (fig 3).

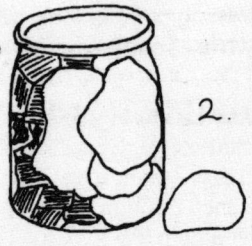

BEADS FROM PAPIER MÂCHÉ

YOU WILL NEED

- paper pulp
- board on which to work
- a packet of cocktail sticks
- paint and brush
- clear nail varnish
- shirring elastic

INSTRUCTIONS

1 Take a piece of pulp in your hand and roll it on the board into a ball. If it looks too big to be a bead then try a smaller piece. Experiment until you have a piece the right size (fig 1).

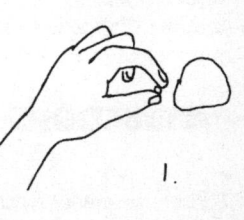

2 Take lots of pieces of pulp the same size, so your beads will be of a uniform size, and roll them into balls (fig 2).

3 Very carefully, push a cocktail stick through the centre of each ball and leave them to dry. You must push the stick through gently, as it is very easy to break up the pulp (fig 3).

4 When the beads are nearly dry remove the cocktail sticks (fig 4).

5 Let the drying process finish and then decorate each bead by painting it (fig 5).

6 Varnish the beads and leave to dry once more.

7 Thread on to shirring elastic (fig 6).

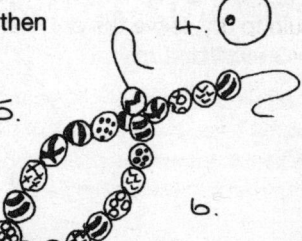

ROLLER PRINT 1

This is a method often used to print fabric commercially.

YOU WILL NEED

- an empty cotton reel
- 2 pencils
- Plasticine
- ink
- poster paint
- sheet of glass or Formica, or an old baking tray.
- paper to print on

INSTRUCTIONS

1 Push the pencil into the cotton reel. If it doesn't fit, hold it in place with some of the Plasticine (fig 1).

2 Cover the cotton reel with a layer of Plasticine and using another pencil mark out a pattern or design (fig 2).

3 Pour the paint into the baking tray or on to the sheet of glass.

4 Roll the cotton reel in the paint and then roll it on to the paper and your design will emerge (fig 3).

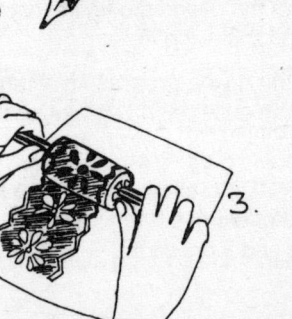

ROLLER PRINT 2

This method of printing is a little more difficult than the first.

YOU WILL NEED

- the cardboard middle of a toilet roll
- a piece of card
- pencil
- glue
- knitting needle or a skewer
- tape measure
- piece of felt or thin sponge
- scissors
- paint
- tin to roll out the paint
- paper on which to print

INSTRUCTIONS

1 Stand the cardboard cylinder on end and draw round the circumference twice, on to the piece of card (fig 1).

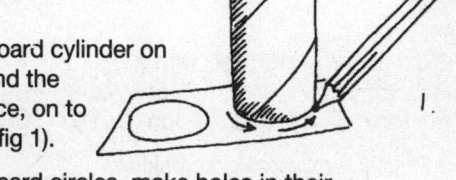

2 Cut out the two card circles, make holes in their centres (fig 2) and then stick them on either end of the cardboard cylinder.

3 Push the knitting needle through both holes.

4 Measure the circumference of the cylinder and cut out a piece of felt or sponge of that dimension by the length of the cylinder (in other words, if the cylinder is 10 cm long with a circumference of 8 cm, cut an oblong 10 cm long and 8 cm wide).

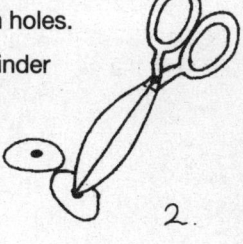

5 Cut out a design on the sponge or felt and then stick the design round the cardboard cylinder (fig 3).

6 Pour out the ink (fig 4) on to the baking tray.

7 Put the roller in the ink and then print the design on the paper.

BRAINWAVE

Instead of felt or sponge use string to make a pattern on your roller.

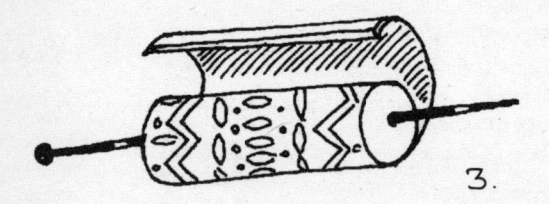

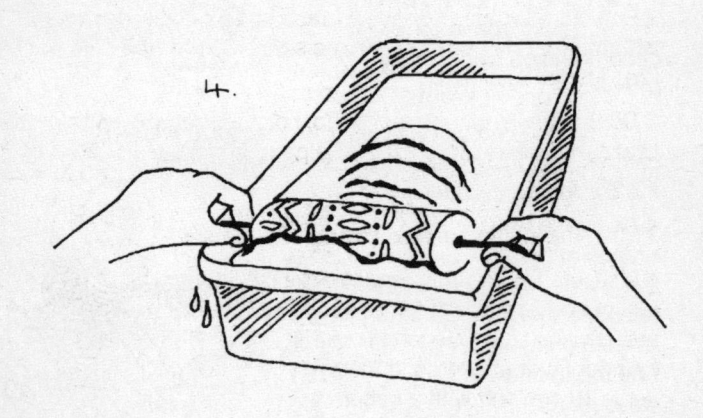

3.

4.

BRASS RUBBING

Brasses are to be found in churches and cathedrals all over England. They are fine examples of the metal-workers' craft between the thirteenth and seventeenth centuries. By placing paper over these brasses and rubbing with a wax crayon you can take away a paper image of that brass. But before you begin to do a brass rubbing, you must first ask permission from the priest of the church concerned.

YOU WILL NEED

- a duster
- a large piece of thinnish paper
- masking tape
- wax crayons

INSTRUCTIONS

1 Dust the brass to remove any particles of grime or dirt.

2 Roll out the paper on to the brass and fix it at the corners with masking tape and down the sides if it is a particularly long image.

3 So that you know where to rub, carefully rub the edge of the brass with the duster so that the perimeter line shows.

4 Using the wax crayon rub over the brass. Try and keep the rubbing even in pressure and rub in one direction.

PATTERNING TISSUES USING FELT TIPS

You can create very pretty papers by folding, wetting and colouring paper.

YOU WILL NEED

- soft absorbent tissue paper (as you use for blowing your nose)
- white paper
- paper towels or kitchen paper
- non-waterproof felt tip pens
- water in a saucer

INSTRUCTIONS

1 Fold a tissue to form a square or triangular wad (fig 1).

2 Wet the tissue wad thoroughly and then blot it between two pieces of kitchen paper.

3 Lay the tissue wad on top of the white paper.

4 Draw on the top layer of the tissue wad with a dotting action – this will deposit lots of ink and will not tear the tissue in the way that drawing lines would.

5 Cover the tissue wad with white paper and press down. The design on the top layer of tissue paper will transfer to the layers beneath.

6 Very carefully unfold the wad and reveal the pattern (fig 2).

7 Leave the piece of tissue to dry. When completely dry, press with a very cool iron.

8 If using for gift wrapping, first cover your present in white paper, as the tissue is flimsy and may show any patterns which are underneath it.

MAKING A COLLAGE

A paper collage is a collection of paper put together in a pleasing way to form a decorative or representational image.

The word collage comes from the French verb "coller" which means to stick. You can collect together a combination of old papers such as stamps, wrapping paper, magazines, bits of corrugated paper etc. You can use new papers, including gift wrap, tissue, crêpe or coloured papers or a combination of old and new. A very famous artist called Kurt Switters used to collect rubbish from the street which he then used to put together to make very interesting collages. Henri Matisse, at the end of his life when he could no longer paint, made many paper collages of figures and plant forms.

Depending on what you are making you can stick the paper down completely or leave parts of it free. For example, by ripping tiny bits of paper you can form feathers on a bird.

One idea for collage is to collect together all the paraphernalia from your holiday – postcards, bus or train tickets, receipts – and put them together to make a picture.

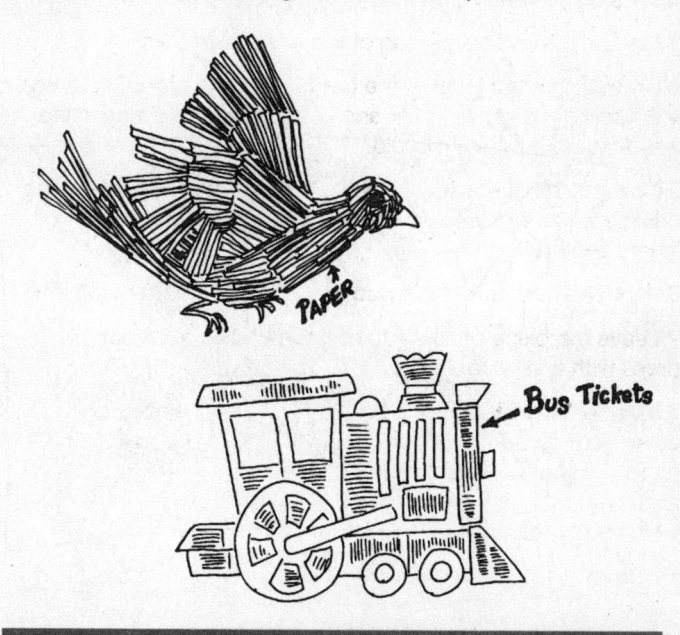

YOU WILL NEED

- paper of many sorts
- glue
- scissors (optional – you often get a more pleasing effect by tearing than cutting)
- a piece of paper on which to make your collage

INSTRUCTIONS

1 Arrange the shapes on your paper until you have a pleasing composition.

2 Lift one piece at a time, glue the back and then stick it into place to make the collage.

BLOCK PRINTS

The first kind of printing you ever did was probably finger prints in school, so you may feel that as a technique it is too babyish for you! But as with all methods of decoration it is not the technique, but how you use it that counts.

FUNNY FOOTSTEPS
This is a fun way to decorate some paper and you could even cut them out and stick them on your wall.

YOU WILL NEED

- lots of newspaper to cover the ground
- a large sheet of paper on which to print
- masking tape
- black poster paint
- saucer
- brush
- somewhere to wash your feet

INSTRUCTIONS

1 Remove your shoes and socks
2 Put plenty of newspaper over the floor.
3 Stick the paper on which you wish to print on to the newspaper with masking tape.
4 Pour the paint into the saucer and then, using the brush, cover the bottom of your feet with black paint.
5 Stand on the paper and transfer the paint from your foot to the paper.
6 Stand on the newspaper and paint the bottom of your feet again, repeat step 6.
7 Carry on until there is a line of footprints travelling up the paper.
8 Wash your feet and clear up!

POTATO PRINTS

Making blocks for printing from potatoes is easy and convenient. However you need to do all your printing on one day as the potatoes may soften and be of no use the following day.

Keep to simple shapes such as a diagonal line or a triangle or a cross. Many patterns may be achieved by turning a block through 90 degrees and printing a line in another direction.

YOU WILL NEED

- potato
- felt tip or pencil
- craft or kitchen knife
- kitchen paper
- printing ink (poster paint or water colour)
- saucer
- paint brush
- paper on which to print

INSTRUCTIONS

1 Wash the potato and cut it in half (fig 1).

2 With the felt tip, draw the design on the flat side of one half of the potato (fig 2).

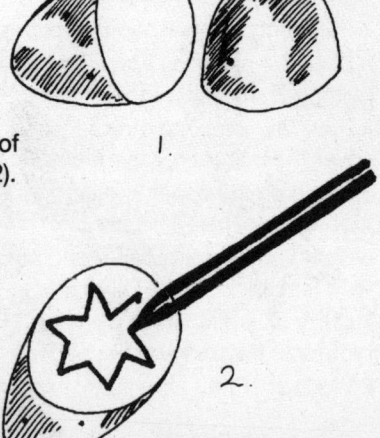

3 With the craft or kitchen knife, cut away the bits surrounding the design so that the image stands proud of the potato.

4 Dab off any excess starch with kitchen paper.

5 Pour the paint into a saucer.

6 With the brush, apply the paint to the design (fig 3) and when it is covered, use the block to print.

7 As the print becomes more faded add more ink to the block.

IDEAS Use other vegetables and fruits cut in half to make patterns, but instead of cutting out a design just use the shape of the half fruit, such as a pear or an apple as the design.

WOODEN BLOCK PRINTS

Blocks for printing can be made from anything with a raised surface which will leave a pattern when ink is applied to it. So you can make prints from the rim of an egg cup, pasta, string or seed stuck on a wooden block.

TO MAKE A BLOCK YOU WILL NEED

- a small block of wood (large enough to be held in the hand)
- strong glue
- string or pasta

INSTRUCTIONS

1 Arrange the pasta or string on the block to create a pleasing pattern.

2 Stick the pieces into place.

3 When the glue has dried use the block in the way you would a potato block.

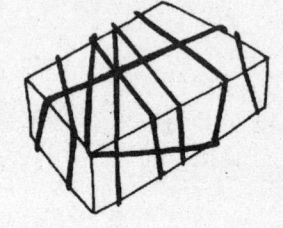

BRAINWAVE

Carve blocks from old wine bottle corks. Use nails in a wooden block to create a pattern.

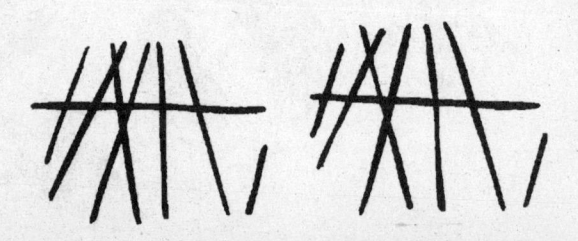

EASY STENCILS

Before making stencils, try some of the following easy techniques to make patterns with very little skill.

PAPER DOILIES

YOU WILL NEED

- a large well-ventilated area in which to work
- newspaper to cover the work area
- paper doilies
- spray paint
- paper on which to print

INSTRUCTIONS

1 Cover your work area in newspaper – spray paint gets every where!

2 Hold the doily on to your paper and spray through it.

3 Remove the doily to reveal the pattern. This makes a lovely lacy effect and is good for gift wrapping.

RIPPED NEWSPAPER

This is easy, as you can rip the newspaper to form abstract patterns and then dab the ink on between the uneven lines.

YOU WILL NEED

- newspaper
- paper on which to print
- sticky tape
- water colour or poster paint in a tube
- saucer
- sponge

INSTRUCTIONS

1 Rip the newspaper along its grain. If the lines are too straight wiggle as you tear to make them less so.

2 Tape the newspaper across the paper on which you are about to print, leaving gaps as you work down the page.

3 Mix up the paint on the saucer.

4 Put the sponge in the paint and then dab any excess off on to spare newspaper.

5 Dab the colour on to the drawing paper between the rows of newspaper (fig 2).

6. Lift up the newspaper to reveal the pattern (fig 3).

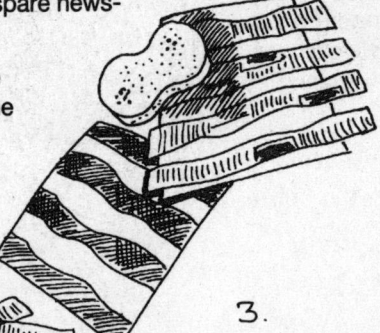

MAKING AND USING STENCILS

Stencils are a way of repeating a design on paper, walls or fabric. The design is held together by "bridges": little bits of whatever the stencil is cut from. When choosing designs, look for things which have obvious bridges, like the spokes on a wheel or segments of an orange.
NOTE If you are cutting your own stencil, get a grown up to help as craft knives can be very sharp.

YOU WILL NEED

- tracing paper
- pencil
- carbon paper
- black felt tip pen
- either manilla paper, vinyl or clear acetate (from which to make the stencil). You can of course practise with a paper stencil first but it won't last for very long.
- board on which to cut
- craft knife
- masking tape
- paper on which to print
- paint
- stencil brush

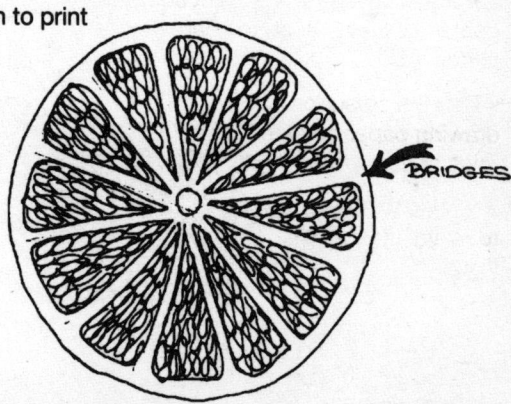

INSTRUCTIONS

1 Trace the design on to tracing paper.

2 Transfer the design by placing a piece of carbon paper between the traced design and the stencil paper. Go over the design with a pen. Remove the tracing paper and carbon and define the marks left on the stencil paper with a black felt tip pen.

3 Tape the stencil paper to the cutting board with masking tape. Using a craft knife cut out the design using a firm, fluent movement. It is easier to move the paper and keep the knife still on the curved parts.

TO PRINT

1 Masking tape the paper on which you are going to print to a flat working surface.

2 Masking tape the stencil on top of the paper. If you are going to make lots of images on the paper, mark where you want them to go before you start printing.

3 Pour the poster paint into a saucer.

4 Make sure the brush is dry. Dip it into the paint and then using an up and down motion stamp off any surplus ink onto newspaper. Only use small amounts of paint at any one time or you will find that it bleeds under the edge of the stencil. This will cause smudging.

5 Hold the stencil in place, with one hand and the brush vertically in the other. Stamp the paint on to the paper with an up and down motion.

For a shaded effect start with the palest colours first and build up to stronger colours.

LINO PRINTING

A lino print is a cut image, made with lino tools. These are special tools with a wooden handle at one end and a blade at the other. However, unlike stencils, you do not cut completely through the lino. The block is still complete but with a series of depressions and raised images.

Lino cuts look very like wood cuts. Like stencils, you draw your design on to tracing paper and trace it off on to the lino but when you carve out the design, the mixture of thick and thin lines, space and texture, will make the lino cut richer. The raised surfaces left by the cutting are then covered in ink and pressed on to paper. If you are going to use the lino many times, it is worth sticking it on a wooden block. The print is the reverse or a mirror image of your block. It is very important to remember it is a mirror image, especially when printing numbers or letters.

LINO CUT

YOU WILL NEED

- newspaper
- drawing paper
- pencil
- tracing paper
- lino
- lino cutters or craft knife
- printing roller
- piece of glass or a smooth flat surface
- printing ink
- printing paper
- masking tape

optional
- wood and wood glue
- wooden mallet

1 Cover your work space in newspaper. Draw the design on paper (fig 1).

2 Trace over the design and then reverse the tracing paper and go over the back of the line you have drawn in pencil.

3 Turn the tracing paper right way round and place it over the lino. Draw again over the design, and the pencil lines on the back will transfer on to the lino.

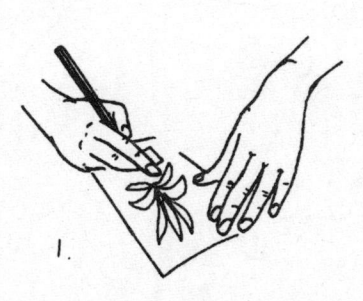

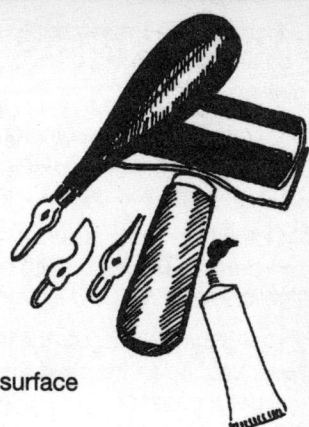

4 Remove the tracing paper and cut out over the lines. When you are trying to cut curves, turn the lino and keep the tool still in your hand.

5 If you are making a block to keep, cut a piece of plywood or soft wood the same dimensions as the lino. Using woodglue, glue the lino on to the mount and leave to dry.

6 Using the rubber roller, roll out the ink on to a piece of glass or Formica. The ink should be thinly and evenly spread, so that the roller neither sticks nor slides (fig 2).

7 Using the roller apply the ink to the block. Do not lift the roller until it has travelled the whole length of the block or you will get a break or inconsistencies in the paint (fig 3).

8 When the block is covered in ink it is time to print. If there is ink on any of the places that you have cut away where you do not want ink, you must rub it off with a cloth.

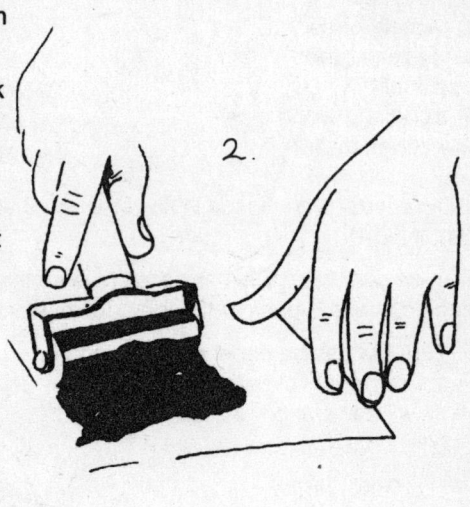

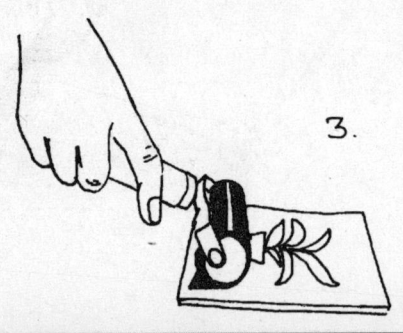

9 Place the paper on which you are going to print face upwards on the table. Secure it at the corners with masking tape. Place the block ink side down on the paper and either run a clean roller firmly over the back of the lino, or, if the lino is on a wood block using a wooden mallet hit the back of the block (fig 4).

10 Lift up the lino and check the image (fig 5).

11 Repeat steps 7-10 for the next print.

12 Wash all the tools and lino block in warm soapy water.

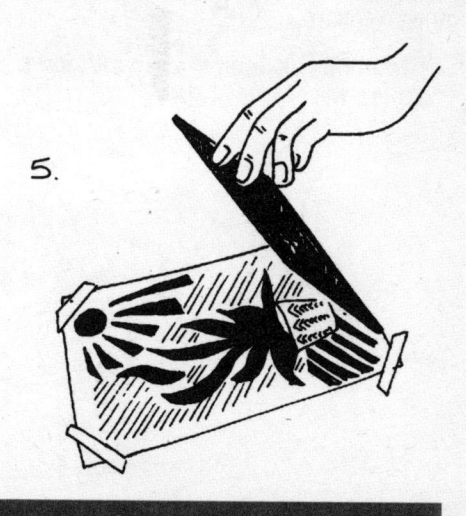

4.

5.

MARBLING PAPER

You can make very pretty paper by marbling, which can be used to make decorations or gift wrap, covering books or many other things.

YOU WILL NEED

- lots of newspaper
- oil based paints (artists' oil paints are fine)
- turpentine substitute
- as many saucers or lids as there are colours
- a bowl of water that is large enough to float the paper on
- brush
- rubber gloves
- plain white paper (typing paper is good)

INSTRUCTIONS

1 Cover your work surface with lots of newspaper. Marbling is fun and very messy! You also need somewhere to put all the finished work whilst it is drying.

2 Squeeze out a little colour on to a saucer and mix with a little turpentine.

3 Drop the colour on to the surface of the water, where it will float (fig 1).

4 Mix a second colour with the first and add it to the first colour. Stir it with the back of the paint brush. Another way of making a pattern is to blow the paint across the surface of the water (fig 2).

5 Put on the rubber gloves to protect your hands. Holding the paper by the corners put it on the surface of the water. The paint will stick to the paper.

6 Lift the paper off quickly so the pattern doesn't run (fig 3).

7 Leave to dry.

8 Add more colours to the water and repeat steps 2-7. Clean all brushes and utensils with turpentine.

2.

3.

DECORATING PAPER BY THE USE OF TEXTURES

With the use of water colour on paper and a variety of unusual things you can create beautiful patterns.

YOU WILL NEED

- poster or water colour paint and a saucer to put it in
- a wide brush for painting
- paper

optional

One or a combination of the things below each will produce a different texture:

- a cork
- sponge
- kitchen paper
- newspaper
- old comb
- old toothbrush
- piece of knitted fabric
- feather
- teddy bear or rabbit pastry cutter
- coloured felt tips

INSTRUCTIONS

CORK PATTERN

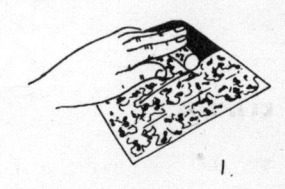

1 Paint the colour on to the paper with the large brush.

2 When the paint is nearly dry, take a cork and roll it over the paper. It will leave a mottled surface pattern (fig 1).

SPONGE PATTERN

1 Using the paint brush cover the paper with paint.

2 Take a dry sponge and dab it in the paint; as you do so colour will lift off.

SPONGE PATTERN 2

This way of making a pattern with a sponge is the reverse of the one above.

1 Pour some paint into a lid or saucer, put the sponge in it and dab it on to the paper (fig 2).

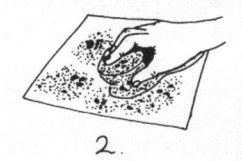

2 For interest add another colour.

KITCHEN ROLL

1 Cover the sheet of paper in paint.

2 Press a sheet of kitchen roll into the paint. As you lift the kitchen roll a pattern will emerge (fig 3).

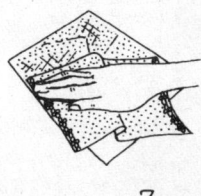

FLICKING

You will need to cover your work area with lots of newspaper as flicked paint gets everywhere!

1 Dip your paint brush in colour and flick it on to the sheet of paper (fig 4).

2 Change brushes for different thicknesses of blobs and change colours to add interest.

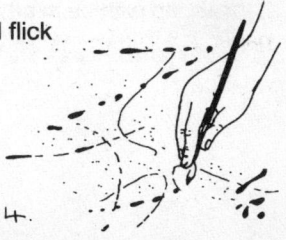

COMBING

1 Cover the paper with paint.

2 Take a comb and drag it through the wet paint. Be careful not to press too hard or you will rip the paper (fig 5).

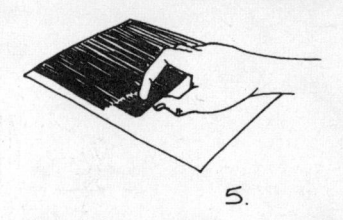

BRAINWAVE

Use an old toothbrush in the same way.

KNITTED FABRIC

Use the sleeve off an old sweater or an old knitted glove (ask permission first!).

1 Dip the sleeve in the paint and dab it on the paper; the knitted pattern will emerge.

BRAINWAVE

Do the same with a feather.

PASTRY CUTTER STENCIL

1 Draw round the cutter on to the paper in pencil.

2 Join the shapes together with lines of colours interweaving with each other.

3 Colour in the shapes and add faces.

PAPER CUTS

Papercuts are a traditional way of creating pictures which look like symmetrical silhouettes, and are found in many countries including Vietnam, China, Mexico, Poland and other parts of Europe. The people who worked in this craft in the past drew their inspiration from the world around them so the pictures included flowers, animals, people and their past times.

The materials you need for this craft are few but the skill involved can be very great.

YOU WILL NEED

- squared paper
- pencil
- sharpener
- some small pointed paper cutting scissors (nail scissors are fine, but ask permission first)
- black paint

INSTRUCTIONS

1 Paint the back of the squared paper black. This will be the front of the design when you have finished your piece of work.

2 Draw a line down the middle of the squared paper, then draw your design on one side of that line (fig 1). Make sure your pencil is sharp so that the design will be crisp. That way it will be easier to make it symmetrical.

3 Fold the paper in half lengthways, with the drawing on the outside.

4 Cut out the design through both layers of paper, making sure not to break it in any places.

5 Unfold and turn the paper over (fig 2).

6 Mount the cut-out on to white paper and then frame it or stick it on the wall.

DECOUPAGE

Sticking paper on to other things as a way of decoration is known as decoupage. It is a very easy way to create an interesting decorative finish without having to be a brilliant artist. It is very good for small items such as boxes, cartons, calendars and greeting cards.

YOU WILL NEED

- box or carton on which to stick (collect old cereal packets, shoe boxes etc)
- unless you are going to cover the item all over with paper cut outs, you will need to give it a coat of paint first; poster is usually opaque enough
- either paper cut outs (sometimes can be bought as ready gummed) or paper, glue and scissors
- varnish

INSTRUCTIONS

1 Paint your box or carton and leave it to dry. If you can still see print underneath give it a second coat.

2 Cut out your shapes. Use those below as a guide – keep them simple but brightly coloured.

3 Stick the shapes into place

4 For protection cover with a coat of clear varnish.

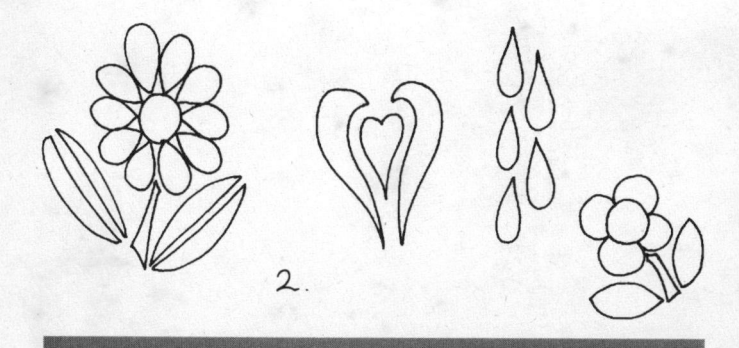

SILHOUETTES

The silhouette was invented by an eighteenth-century minister of finance called Etienne de Silhouette whose hobby was cutting out profiles in paper.

YOU WILL NEED

- a model
- a chair
- a sheet of thin white paper
- drawing pins
- a slide projector or an unshaded electric light with a clear bulb
- a pencil or a felt tip pen
- tracing paper
- a sheet of black or coloured cartridge paper
- sharp scissors

INSTRUCTIONS

1 Seat the model on the chair in a dark room as near to the wall as possible, with his or her profile parallel to the wall.

2 Pin the white paper to the wall behind the model.

3 Place the light on the other side of the model adjusting it until a shadow falls on the paper (fig 1).

1.

4 Trace around the silhouette with the pencil or felt tip.

5 Trace the profile on to black paper, then cut it out and stick into position on white paper (fig 2).

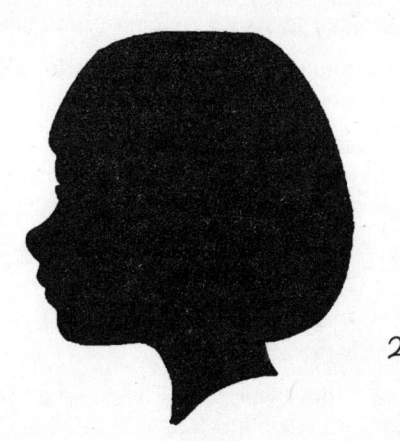

2.

MASKS FROM PAPER PLATES

Paper plates are very easy for making masks of many different kinds.

YOU WILL NEED

- a paper plate for each mask
- pencil
- scissors
- shirring elastic and needle
- paper or thin card for ears etc
- egg boxes for noses
- glue or stapler
- paint or felt tips

INSTRUCTIONS

1 Work out your design on paper.

2 Hold up the plate against your face and very carefully, with a pencil, mark where your eyes come.

3 Parallel with the eye marks and about 2cm (³/₄ in) from one edge of the plate, pierce a hole, and tie on the shirring elastic.

4 Make sure that you have enough elastic to hold the plate comfortably on to your head, and then make a hole 2cm (³/₄ in) from the edge on the opposite side of the plate.

5 Cut out noses, hair, ears, whiskers etc, and stick them into place.

6 Make animal markings for a tiger or zebra, or paint for a clown's face, elephant, rabbit or cat.

7 You can cut away the lower part of the mask and add fangs for a frightening tiger or lion mask.

PAPIER MÂCHÉ HELMET

From this one method you can make masks and helmets of many varieties.

YOU WILL NEED

- tape measure
- balloon
- thread and button or matchstick
- funnel and bottle
- masking tape
- wallpaper paste
- newspaper
- paint in gold or silver or black

INSTRUCTIONS

1 Measure the circumference of the head of the person who will wear the helmet.

2 Blow up the balloon to slightly larger than this measurement; this will allow for shrinkage and for ease when putting on.

3 Tie a button or matchstick to the thread. Pass the other end of the thread through the funnel and tie it to the balloon. The matchstick or button will keep the balloon in place in the funnel whilst you work (fig 1).

4 Tape the tube of the funnel in to the bottle.

5 Mix up the wallpaper paste according to the makers' instructions.

6 Rip the newspaper into strips, dip them in the glue and lay in overlapping strips over the balloon until its surface is completely covered. Leave to dry.

7 Repeat step six a further five times, until you have a thick strong helmet shape (fig 2).

8 Remove the balloon from the funnel and bottle and either prick the balloon or pull it out if it has deflated.

9 To make a helmet cut away the front (fig 3).

10 Add a yoghurt pot to the top of the helmet (fig 4) and a plume to the yoghurt pot (fig 5) and paint the helmet.

11 To make masks cut the papier mâché in half lengthways (fig 6). Cut holes for eyes and buildup features with cardboard or Plasticine and paint.

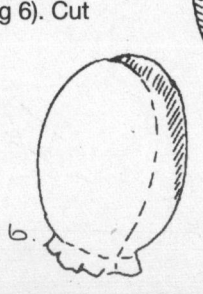

PAPER COSTUMES

Fancy dress can be very expensive. Paper is a good cheap material for making costumes, but it is not particularly durable except in the form of papier mâché or cardboard.

SOLDIER COSTUME

Make epaulettes which can be worn on your school blazer. Cover the buttons in *washed* milk bottle tops and make a row of medals to wear on your chest.

TO MAKE EPAULETTES

YOU WILL NEED

- cardboard from a cereal packet
- yellow crêpe paper
- glue
- string
- gold paint
- 25cm (10 in) of sticky-backed velcro

INSTRUCTIONS

1 Cut two oval shapes from the cardboard (fig 1), big enough to fit on the shoulders of your blazer.

2 Cut enough crêpe paper to go all the way round the oval and 5cm (2 in) deep. This is for the fringing on the epaulette. Cut the paper to within 5mm (¼ in) of the end to form the fringe (fig 2) and stick it into place.

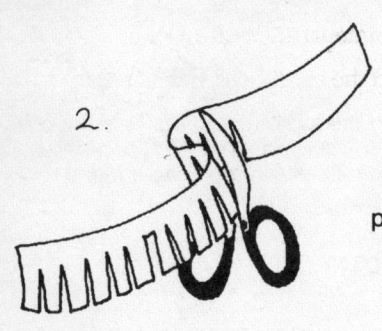

3 Wind some string round the edge of the cardboard, covering the edge of the fringing, and add some to the middle in the form of a pattern (fig 3). Stick into place.

4 Paint the cardboard and string with gold paint and leave to dry.

Step 4 is optional as you can balance the epaulettes on your jacket or blazer.

5 Cut the sticky-back velcro in half. Stick one side to the underside of each epaulette and the other to your blazer. It should come off when you need to remove it.

TO MAKE MEDALS

YOU WILL NEED

- cardboard
- scissors
- felt tips
- striped ribbon or material you can colour with felt tips
- large safety pin

INSTRUCTIONS

1 Cut out the shape below in card (fig 1).

2 Decorate with felt tips.

3 Cut a piece of ribbon or material 20cm (8 in) long.

4 Decorate the material and the cardboard with felt tips.

5 Thread the ribbon through the top of the medal and pin on to your costume (fig 2).

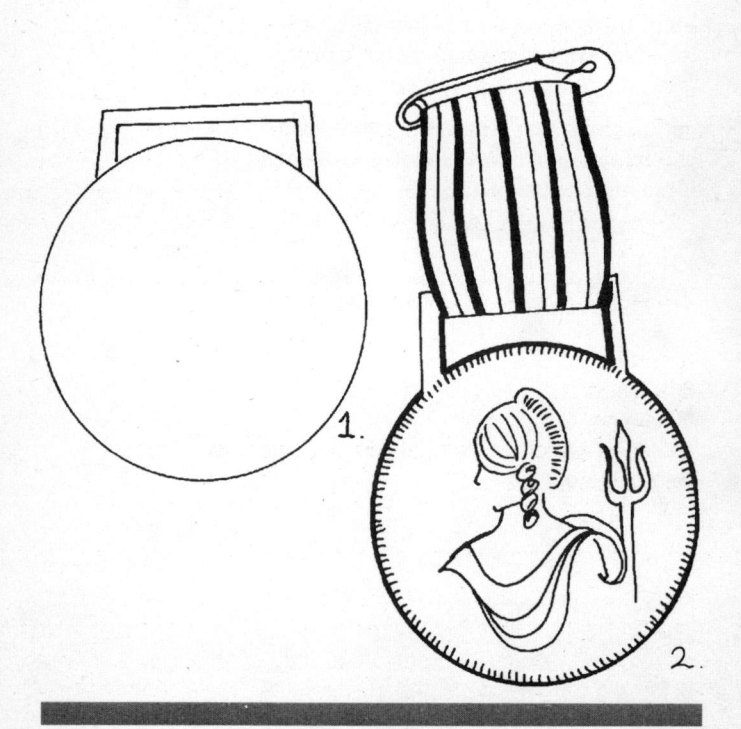

SHIELDS

Shields and axes and spears can all be made from cardboard. For the axe and spear you will need an old broom handle.

YOU WILL NEED

- washing powder box with a handle
- scissors
- pencil
- glue
- string
- tin foil
- black shoe polish
- for the spear or axe, a broomstick

INSTRUCTIONS

1 Cut the front of the box off for your shield (fig 1). Retain the lid with the handle.

2 Draw the shape you want your shield to be – round, oval or any shape you like – on to the front of the box (fig 2).

3 Cut out the shield shape.

4 Stick the handle to the centre of the back of the shield. This is the part you will hold on to (fig 3).

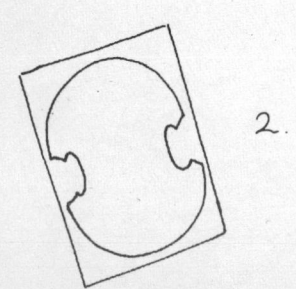

5 Decorate the front of the shield by sticking the string on in patterns (fig 4).

6 Cut a piece of tin foil slightly larger than the shield shape and smooth it over the string covered shield so that the pattern shows through the foil.

7 Antique the surface of the shield by rubbing in black shoe polish.

Make a spear or an axe by cutting out the shape in card, attaching it to a broom stick with glue or sticky tape and decorating as you did the shield (fig 5).

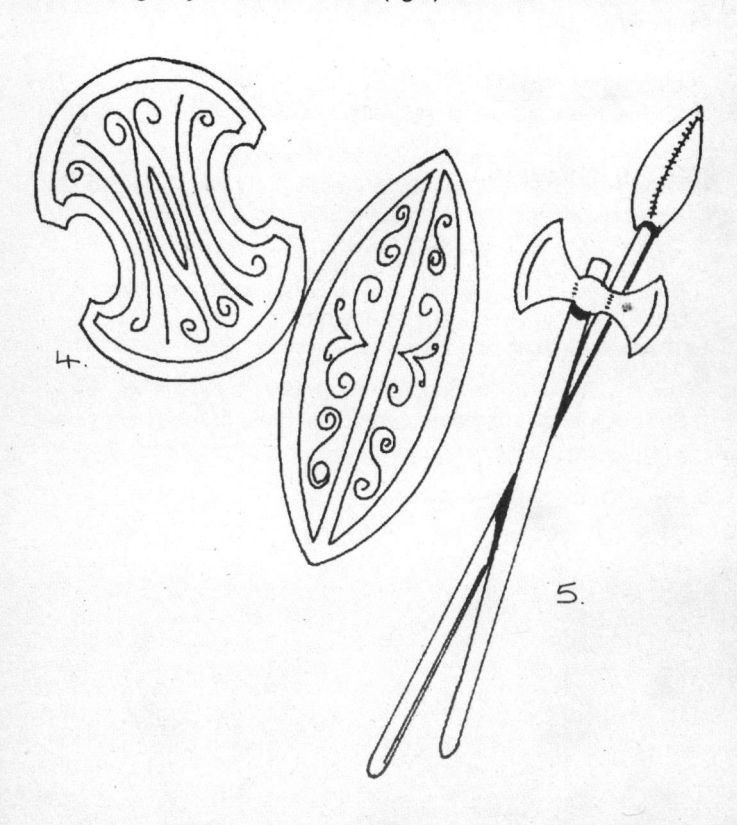

BOOK PLATES

Book plates are labels which you stick in the front of a book to show that it belongs to you. They usually have a decorative motif such as a cat, a bear, or books on them, as well as room for the name of the person to whom the book belongs.

YOU WILL NEED

- a packet of plain gummed labels
- pens, crayons or felt tips
- tracing paper and pencil

INSTRUCTIONS

1 Draw or stencil your design on to the label, leaving room for the person's name. You may prefer to draw your design on to tracing paper and then to trace it off on to each label.

2 Write either THIS BOOK BELONGS TO :
or the same in Latin, which is EX LIBRIS, on to each label.

BRAINWAVES

You may like to make decorative labels in the same way for a keen cook to put on homemade preserves, or for a handyman to put on containers for storing nails and other items.

PAPER FLOWERS

Paper flowers can be a lovely present for someone, especially in the winter. The ones below are easy to make as they are made from ordinary paper tissues.

YOU WILL NEED

- white and pink tissues
- scissors
- milliners' or florists' wire

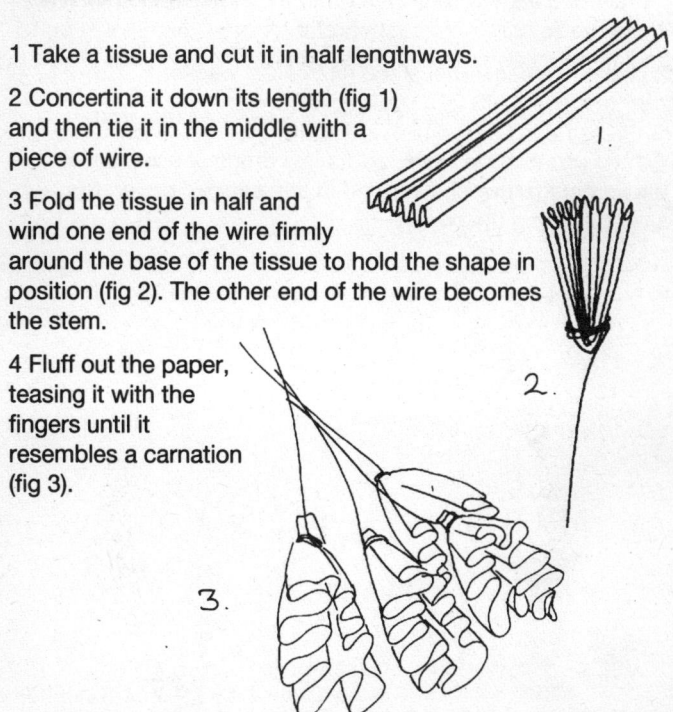

INSTRUCTIONS

1 Take a tissue and cut it in half lengthways.

2 Concertina it down its length (fig 1) and then tie it in the middle with a piece of wire.

3 Fold the tissue in half and wind one end of the wire firmly around the base of the tissue to hold the shape in position (fig 2). The other end of the wire becomes the stem.

4 Fluff out the paper, teasing it with the fingers until it resembles a carnation (fig 3).

PERFUMED PAPERS

This is a wonderful present. You can perfume all kinds of papers from gift wrap and drawer liners to stationery and boxes.

YOU WILL NEED

- a large plastic box (such as tupperware) in which to hold the paper products
- paper of various sorts, writing paper, envelopes etc
- pot pourri sachets or lavender bags

INSTRUCTIONS

1 Place the papers and the pot pourri sachet in the box and close the lid.

2 Leave in a dark, cool place for several weeks.

3 Remove the paper and use or give away as required.

4 If the scent is too weak, add a few drops of essential oil to a piece of cotton wool, wrapped in greaseproof paper; this will stop it staining the paper.

CAT PENCIL HOLDER

This is a useful desk tidy.

YOU WILL NEED

- a piece of medium weight card, 30.5cm (12 in) long
- felt tips for eyes and nose
- some strips of coloured card or paper for whiskers
- scissors and glue

INSTRUCTIONS

1 Following the diagram, draw the cat shape on the card and cut it out (fig 1).

2 Make criss-cross slits where the pencils will be held.

3 Cut along the solid line of the tail but leave it attached at the dotted line.

4 Fold along the dotted line and bend the tail back behind the cat.

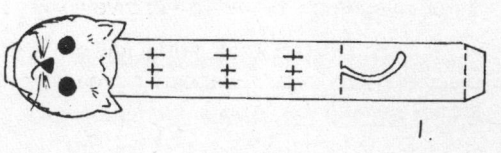

5 Glue flap A behind the cat's nose (fig 2).

6 Colour in the eyes and nose.

7 Stick on the paper or card whiskers.

8 Load pencils (fig 3).

CHRISTMAS CARDS

Making your own cards is always more fun than buying them. Here are a few ideas.

STAINED GLASS WINDOW

YOU WILL NEED

- black card approximately 21cm x 15cm (8 in x 6 in).
- scissors
- tissue paper
- glue – Pritt stick is ideal
- an envelope for the finished card

INSTRUCTIONS

1 Fold the card in half so it is 10.5cm x 15cm (4 in x 6 in)(fig 1).

2 Draw a design on to one side of the card. The more simple the design the easier it will be to cut out. Remember when cutting, it is the bits with the holes that you are keeping not the bits you cut away (fig 2).

3 Cut a piece of tissue paper 10.5cm x 15cm (4 in x 6 in).

4 Dab glue on the back of the card round where you have cut out and stick the tissue paper on to the back of the cut out (fig 3). Leave to dry.

5 As you get more skilled, use different coloured tissue papers for different areas so that it looks like a real stained glass window.

MERRY CHRISTMAS CARD

YOU WILL NEED

- some shiny card 21cm x 30cm (8 in x 12 in)
- glittery thread and a darning needle
- glue

INSTRUCTIONS

1 Cut the card into two pieces 21cm x 15cm (8 in x 6 in)

2 Thread the glittery yarn on to the darning needle. Tie a knot in the end of the thread.

3 Bend both pieces of card into two pieces 10.5cm x 15cm (4 in x 6 in) so that they will stand up (fig 1).

4 Sew from the back of one piece of card the words MERRY CHRISTMAS (fig 2).

5 Stick the second piece of card on the inside of the first so that the wool and the knot are covered (fig 3).

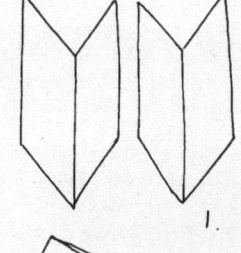

THREE-DIMENSIONAL CHRISTMAS TREE CARD

YOU WILL NEED

- pencil and tracing paper
- green card
- scissors
- glue
- glitter

INSTRUCTIONS

1 Trace off the tree on the following page.

2 Transfer on to two pieces of card and cut the shape out.

3 Cut a slit from the top to the centre point on one card and from the bottom to the centre point on the other piece of card.

4 Dab spots of glue on to one side of each tree shape and sprinkle with glitter. Leave to dry.

5 When the cards are dry turn them over and repeat step 4

6 To make a three-dimensional tree, slot the two pieces of card together.

105

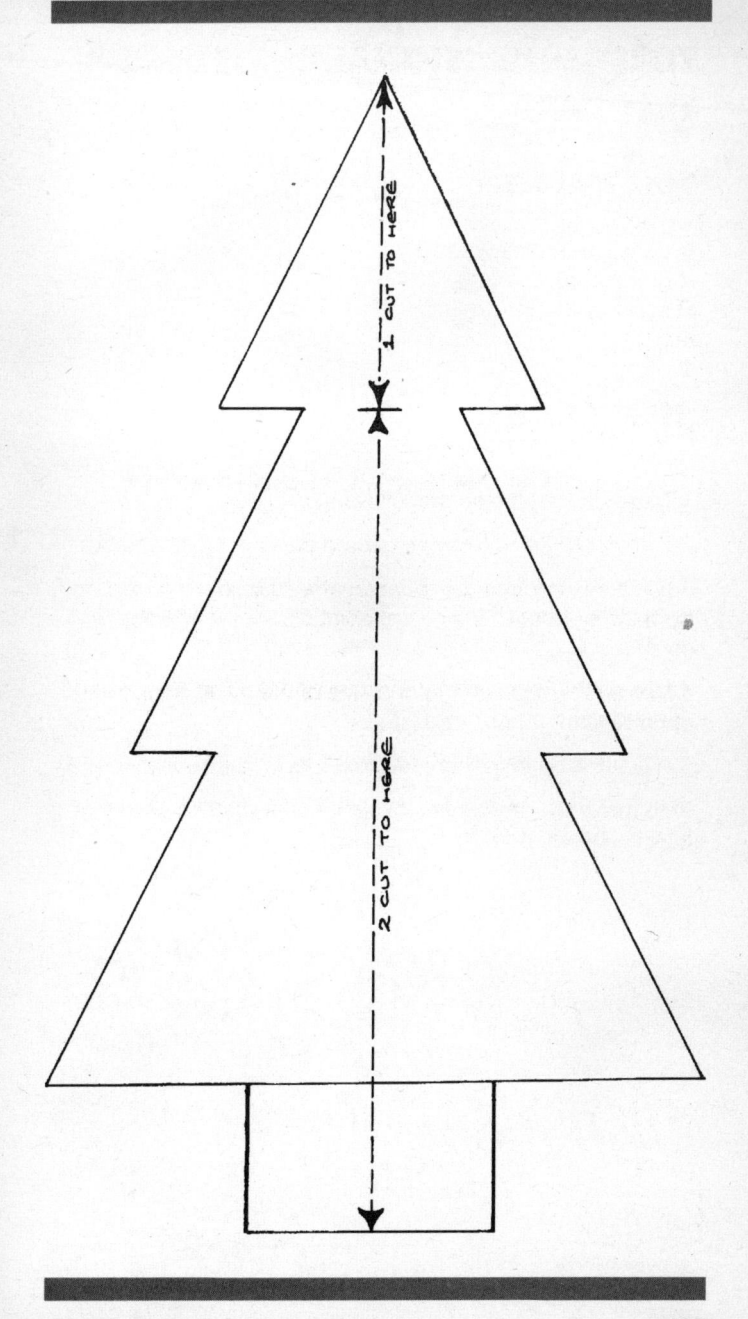

PAPER HATS

YOU WILL NEED

- tape measure or a piece of string and felt tips
- tissue paper
- scissors
- pencil
- ruler
- glue stick

INSTRUCTIONS

1 Measure your head with the tape measure or with the piece of string and mark the string with a dot. Add 5cm (2 in) overlap (this is for sticking).

2 Cut a strip of tissue paper to the length of your head measurement plus the 5cm. The height can be whatever you wish this will vary according to the design that you are using.

3 Draw your design on to the tissue paper using a pencil and ruler and cut it out.

4 Stick the ends together and adjust to fit.

5 If you wish to, colour it in using felt tips. Below are some ideas for hat shapes.

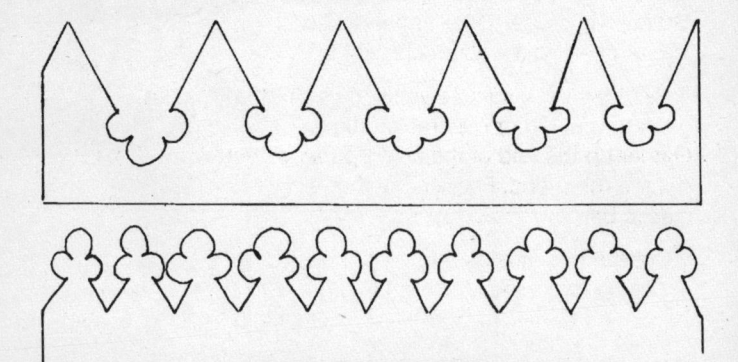

PAPER CRACKERS

Make your own crackers for birthday or Christmas events or even as gifts.

YOU WILL NEED

- crêpe paper
- scissors
- toilet roll middle
- glue
- two small rubber bands
- a joke written on a small piece of paper
- small sweets ar gifts
- tissue paper hat (p106)
- doily
- old magazines

INSTRUCTIONS

1 Cut the crêpe paper so that it is 10cm (4 in) longer than the toilet roll holder.

2 Place the toilet roll holder in the middle of the crêpe paper and glue it into place (fig 1).

3 Fold the crêpe paper round the toilet roll holder until it completly covers the card. Gather the crêpe paper at one end of the roll and secure it with an elastic band.

4 Drop the joke, some sweets, a hat and gift into the end of the cracker (fig 2). Gather up the end of the crêpe paper as you did the other end. Fasten together with an elastic band.

5 Cut out bits of doily, old magazines etc to decorate the cracker (fig 3).

WRAP IT UP

Unusual gift-wrapping ideas.

ENVELOPE

Rather than a predictable flat package, why not make use of the shape of your gift; make an envelope for your LP or compact disc so that it looks like a large card.

YOU WILL NEED

- a large piece of paper, about twice the size of your LP or compact disc.
- pencil
- ruler
- craft knife
- Copydex or other glue
- if your paper is a pastel colour, buy a felt tip or crayon of the same colour but a shade darker

INSTRUCTIONS

1 Place your LP in the centre of the paper and draw round it with a pencil.

2 Remove the LP and add 2mm ($^1/_{10}$ in) all the way round the first line to allow the LP to fit into the envelope when it is finished.

3 Using the ruler, draw flaps as indicated on the diagram (fig 1).

4 Cut the complete envelope out and fold in the side flaps. Then fold up the bottom flap. Stick the bottom flap on to the side flaps. Fold down but do not stick the top flap. Insert the LP (fig 2).

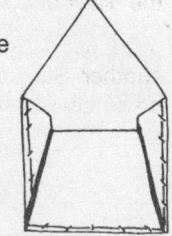

5 Using the coloured pencil, draw a decorative line 5mm (¼ in) from the edge on the back of the envelope.

6 Make a large stamp and cut the edge with pinking shears if you have them, or make a zigzag edge with ordinary scissors. Stick into place on the front of the envelope and write your message as you would the address.

SNAKES AND LADDERS GAME

You can make a game of snakes and ladders which you can actually play, or any other board game such as backgammon or chess.

YOU WILL NEED

- black paper or cardboard
- scissors
- Fablon
- pencil and ruler

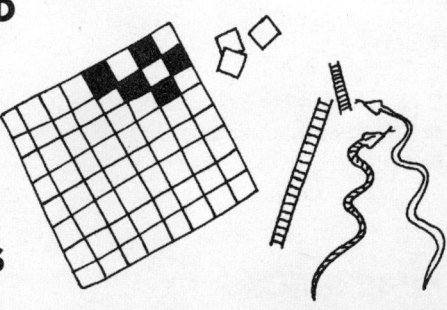

INSTRUCTIONS

1 Make an envelope from black paper, or an outer sleeve like an LP cover, or just cut a square of cardboard.

2 Draw a grid over one side with squares of the same dimensions as 4 squares on the back of the Fablon.

3 Cut out squares from Fablon, peel away the backing paper from each piece and stick them down on alternate squares on the black grid.

4 Cut out snakes from another colour and ladders from yet another. Stick them over the board. If you wish the board to be durable, cover it with a sheet of clear Fablon.

TOP HAT

Bottles are acceptable gifts to most people but they are difficult to make look interesting. How about gift-wrapping your bottle so that it looks like a stove pipe or elongated top hat.

YOU WILL NEED

- black paper
- piece of ribbon or contrasting coloured paper
- glue
- cardboard such as a cereal box

INSTRUCTIONS

1 Make a cylinder from black paper that just fits round the bottle and is slightly taller. Join it together with glue.

2 Cut a circle with a diameter of 5cm (2 in) wider than the cylinder. Cut notches in the circle up to the circumference of the cylinder (fig 1).

3 Bend the notches down and then try the circle for size in the cylinder to see if it fits. If it does, stick it in to the cylinder with the notches facing down (fig 2).

4 Cut three circles for the base and brim with a diameter 10cm (4 in) wider than the cylinder, two of black paper and one of card. Stick one of the black circles on to the card.

5 Cut radiating lines from the centre of the other circle. Place the bottle on the circle brim with the cardboard facing up and the black paper down, and then fit the cut circle over it (fig 3). Put the cylinder on top of that. If it all fits, stick the top circle to the bottom circle and to the sides of the cylinder. Decorate with a ribbon (fig 4).

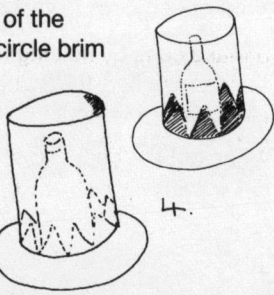

WRAPPING AN AWKWARD SHAPE

Tissue paper in different colours is a pretty solution. If you are wrapping something sharp such as a teapot with a spout then soften it with cotton wool, so that the sharp bits won't protrude.

YOU WILL NEED

- tissue paper of different colours
- ribbon for wrapping
- scissors
- cotton wool

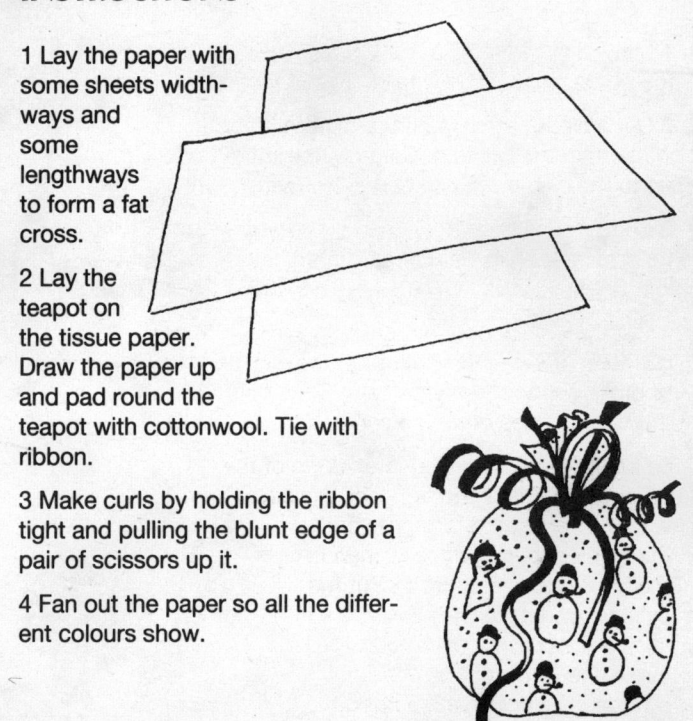

INSTRUCTIONS

1 Lay the paper with some sheets widthways and some lengthways to form a fat cross.

2 Lay the teapot on the tissue paper. Draw the paper up and pad round the teapot with cottonwool. Tie with ribbon.

3 Make curls by holding the ribbon tight and pulling the blunt edge of a pair of scissors up it.

4 Fan out the paper so all the different colours show.

DESIGNER WRAP

If you are stuck why not just wrap your present in brown paper. Either tie with hairy string or gold braid. Tie on a luggage label with your message.

Or put lots of little presents in a clear polythene bag and add bright pictures cut out of magazines in the same shades and some shredded tissue and staple together.

SOCK IT TO THEM

Two unusual ways to give a pair of socks. The first is to cut two shoe shapes (fig 1) and cut a hole in the upper one. Decorate with a shoe lace or ribbon. Stick the upper one to the lower one around the edge and then insert the sock. Push the second sock inside the top of the first to bulk it out and make an ankle (fig 2). Or the second way is to cut a boot shape in profile and roll the sock over the top edge.

MAKING YOUR OWN GIFT WRAP

Potato prints, sponging or stencilling through a doily.